Princeton Theological Seminary

Princeton Theological Seminary

A Narrative History

1812-1992

William K. Selden

Copyright © 1992 William K. Selden

ISBN 0-9634444-0-9 (cloth)
ISBN 0-9634444-1-7 (paper)

Printed by
Princeton University Press

Library of Congress
Cataloging-in-Publication Data

Selden, William K.
Princeton Theological Seminary : a narrative
history, 1812-1992 / William K. Selden.
p.   cm.
Includes bibliographical references and index.
ISBN 0-9634444-0-9
1. Princeton Theological Seminary—History. I. Title.
BV4070-P76S45 1992
230'.5174965—dc20   92-35559

*It is a sound maxim that men living at one time
must not be judged by the maxims of an age in which
all circumstances are greatly changed.*
—Archibald Alexander, 1843

Contents

Illustrations

Foreword

A brief history of Princeton Theological Seminary, concise enough to be read in an evening but comprehensive enough to reward that investment of time, has long been overdue. With the publication of the present volume, that deficiency is rectified.

Recognizing the many dimensions of this institution's life, the author traces the evolving relationships with University and town, with social movements of the nineteenth and early twentieth centuries, and with the sometimes tumultuous development of American Presbyterianism. Although determined not to judge the complex religious and theological questions with which a seminary inevitably becomes associated, he recognizes the importance of these matters for his task and draws upon the work of recognized scholars to provide the necessary commentary.

The book carries us down to the current decade, but the major interpretative thrusts are muted with the Second World War. There is a wealth of archival information for the later period, and native Princetonians will have their own vivid recollections of persons and events. We are too close to these times, however, to read their signs well, and perhaps their interpretation should be left to our successors.

We are grateful to William K. Selden for the enormous labor that has been poured into this work. An educator, author, and community servant of great distinction, he graciously undertook a task certain to be fraught with controversy and produced a volume from which persons inside and outside the Seminary can learn much. His is not, of course, an official or definitive history; the latter is impossible to achieve and the former ought not be attempted. It is, however, a serious work, designed both to give a usable insight into the story of the Seminary and to encourage the interested reader to probe the subject more deeply.

Particularly appropriate would have been a Foreword by Professor Hugh Thomson Kerr. Tim (as he was known by his friends) shared both William Selden's Princeton University pedigree and a devotion to the town where both families resided. He read the manuscript in its earlier stages but was prevented by death from completing the review.

Princeton, New Jersey   *James F. Armstrong*
August 1992   Helena Professor of Old Testament
                               and James Lenox Librarian

Preface

On a cheerful, sunny spring day in 1990 Frederick W. Cassell, Vice President for Seminary Relations, invited me for luncheon at the Nassau Club, originally the home of Samuel Miller, the second professor to be appointed at Princeton Theological Seminary. In view of the fact that on several previous occasions Dr. Cassell had indicated the need for a history of the Seminary, I had a premonition that the meeting was to be more than a social event. When he arrived accompanied by William O. Harris, Librarian for Archives and Special Collections, and Hugh T. Kerr, Jr., Professor of Systematic Theology Emeritus and Editor of *Theology Today*, I realized that my assumptions were correct, and that any protestations of inadequacy on my part for the assignment would be of no avail.

Many months later as I was completing the first draft of this narrative history I found myself subconsciously repeating a quotation the origin of which at the time I did not know. It was from *An Essay on Criticism* by Alexander Pope (1688–1744)—''For fools rush in where angels fear to tread.''

These words have special pertinence in this instance in view of the fact that over a span of a century and a half a succession of theologically erudite Princeton Seminary professors—Samuel Miller, Benjamin B. Warfield, John DeWitt, and Lefferts A. Loetscher—had each been encouraged to undertake this assignment that not one of them had ever completed. Possibly they represented Pope's angels and were wiser than me in not attempting to fill this void.

With my non-theological background I could not have completed the assignment without the assistance of several individuals at the Seminary who were constructive in their suggestions, generous of their time, and gracious in their appreciation that this project was an educational experience for me in many different ways.

Most fortunately I have enjoyed the assistance of a number of individuals who read draft copies of the manuscript, offered excellent suggestions, and corrected some errors that I might otherwise have made. To them I am truly indebted. In this manner, James F. Armstrong, Lenox Librarian, was especially helpful. Likewise, with his extensive historical perspective Mr. Harris read the manuscript and continually gave me encouragement. Others to whom I am indebted for their comments include Thomas W. Gillespie, President of the Seminary, and David B. Watermulder, immediate past Chairman of the Board of Trustees, as well as Dr. Cassell and Professor Kerr, the latter who shared his comments with me only a few days before he died.

James S. Irvine, Associate Seminary Librarian, was more than a copy editor. He also suggested substantive improvements and selections of words that would not encourage possible theological misinterpretations. Henry I. MacAdam, Associate in the Archives and Special Collections, generously assumed the task of preparing the index. They and Marsha L. Roche, Controller, and Katherine A. Skrebutenas, Reference Librarian, never failed to be of help when I needed assistance, which was quite frequent. As with several of my previous publications, Carol Jeffery of the Princeton University Press was an excellent and perceptive facilitator whose discreetly offered comments were received with gratitude.

The knowledge that I acquired from the research that was required and the friendships that were developed in the span of a year and a half made this project a delightful experience for the author.

Princeton, New Jersey   *William K. Selden*
July 1992

xiv

Princeton Theological Seminary

Prologue

Princeton Theological Seminary in the Early 1990s

Located equidistant between the two largest metropolitan regions on the eastern seaboard of the United States, situated in a vibrant university town, nestled among numerous educational institutions extending from kindergarten to post-doctoral and research institutes, Princeton Theological Seminary enjoys an environment that is both congenial and stimulating for the education of future religious leaders. In this final decade of the twentieth century the Seminary continues the never-ending study of the foundation and heritage of Christian beliefs and thought; it pursues its concerns not only for the inadequacies but also for the opportunities of contemporary society, and it conjectures and theorizes on the future salvation of humanity. At Princeton Theological Seminary faculty and students are jointly engaged in the great enterprise of continually improving and strengthening the moral and religious fabric of society.

Men and women of all races with a diversity of over fifty religious denominations are represented in a student body that usually includes representatives from each of the states and some two dozen foreign lands with Korea alone currently providing annually a delegation of over twenty students. In recent years the enrollment has averaged well over eight hundred, more than one-third of whom have been women. The students have entered from a diversity of backgrounds as is attested by their previous education in over four hundred colleges and universities and as many as one hundred seminaries.

To meet the educational needs of a student body with such cultural diversity and divergent vocational goals a curriculum has been developed that now includes nearly 250 courses, some of which are offered in alternate years. These courses are avail-

3

able to students enrolled in the several different degree programs as well as to a few auditors and unclassified students who are admitted each year.

The academic programs for which degrees are offered include the following:

Master of Divinity—a three-year program of biblical, historical, theological, and practical studies basic to any ordained ministry or plan of graduate study.

Master of Arts—a two-year program providing professional preparation for the direction of Christian education in church or secular schools.

Master of Theology—a one-year program in residence plus additional academic work for those engaged in specialized ministries or who wish to increase their competencies in particular areas of parish work.

Master of Divinity-Master of Social Work—a four-year program, including a summer course, which is conducted in cooperation with Rutgers University and which is designed for those who require a background in both theology and social work disciplines.

Doctor of Ministry—a professional program to be completed in three to four years and intended to assist those who are engaged in full-time ministerial and religious educational positions, and which integrates the theological and practical aspects of their ministerial services.

Doctor of Philosophy—a program normally completed within six years intended to prepare men and women for independent scholarship in various dimensions of the study of religion and for teaching in colleges and theological seminaries.

As the largest Presbyterian seminary and one of the largest seminaries of any denomination in the United States, Princeton Theological Seminary supports, in addition to visiting lecturers and clinical supervisors, a full-time faculty of nearly fifty men and women with varied cultural, racial, and theological backgrounds. The physical facilities include sixteen major buildings, all either recently constructed or modernized within the past twelve years, on two adjacent campuses in Princeton, in addition to a large housing complex for married students located

4

within several miles of the community. The Seminary Library, which is in the process of being enlarged, contains a collection of nearly a half million books, monographs, pamphlets and archival items that academicians from around the world value highly in pursuit of their scholarly endeavors.

With its academic and theological traditions maintained by a strong faculty and with the support of its substantial financial and physical assets Princeton Theological Seminary is fully able in the 1990s to fulfill its long-standing statement of purpose.

The purpose of Princeton Theological Seminary is to prepare men and women for able and faithful ministry in the Christian church and present-day society. Committed to a learned ministry for church and society, the Seminary welcomes qualified students without regard to denomination, race, physical handicap, or sex. Through regular chapel worship and other campus functions, the Seminary seeks to strengthen and deepen the spiritual life of students, and through classroom and other academic activities to confront them in critical discussions about the Bible and Christian doctrine with probing questions about faith and life in today's world.

The following narrative history is intended to inform the reader how modern-day Princeton Theological Seminary evolved from an institution which opened in 1812 with one professor, three students, no property, and little money. It is a fascinating tale of devotion to the Christian doctrine of human salvation.

1

From the Beginning

GENESIS

From its early beginnings the Theological Seminary of the Presbyterian Church in the United States of America, as it was initially named, was and has continued to be a significant force in the Reformed tradition of Christianity both in this country and throughout the world. Whereas the date of 1812 identifies the year of the founding of Princeton Theological Seminary, as it has been commonly known, its beginnings can be traced to the early 1700s when William Tennent opened his Log College at Neshaminy in southeastern Pennsylvania. There he, an ordained scholar, born in Ireland and educated at the University of Edinburgh, conducted a school for his sons and more than a dozen other young men, each of whom became leaders in the Great Awakening that burst forth in the middle of the eighteenth century throughout most of the North American colonies.

The term Log College was applied in derision by those who opposed on theological grounds the teachings of Tennent and his evangelical and pietistic approach to religion. The opponents also insisted on what they considered to be more rigorous and appropriate requirements for ordination. Their attacks and the counter-arguments were intimately related to the schism that developed in the colonial Presbyterian church from 1741 to 1758.

In 1746, in an act of protest, the New Siders, as the more evangelical divines were called, established the College of New Jersey, the institution that was later renamed Princeton University. Its primary purpose was to educate young men for the Presbyterian ministry in a more liberal spirit than prevailed at Harvard and Yale colleges, at the time centers of credal orthodoxy.

Scots-Irish Presbyterian Influences

In order to practice their religions as they chose and, in most cases, to improve their economic status, thousands of individuals and their families migrated to the British colonies of North America during the seventeenth and eighteenth centuries. They came from the British Isles in larger numbers but also from France, Germany, the Netherlands, Sweden and Switzerland. Their desire for freedom involved freedom to pursue their religious practices unfettered by political restrictions, restrictions that they themselves often imposed in their new environment on others who did not conform to their beliefs. The early Puritans and later the Congregationalists of New England were notable for their enforcement of prohibitions of other denominational practices. In contrast, under its Quaker influence Pennsylvania was hospitable to those with different religious orientations and it was here that a majority of Presbyterians initially migrated, a large number of whom were Scots emigrating from Ireland. (They are Scots, not Scotch, which is a famous Scottish libation.)

Through the influence of John Knox the Scots-Irish inherited their religious convictions from John Calvin, the primary initiator of the reform movement that subsequently encompassed a number of Protestant denominations. Most importantly, they subscribed to the Westminster Confession of Faith which was produced by an assembly comprised largely of Puritan clergymen convened between 1643 and 1649 by the British Parliament during the protectorship of Oliver Cromwell. This document was adopted at that time by the Church of Scotland and later by the several Presbyterian bodies in North America. It proclaimed that Scripture in the original language is the sole doctrinal authority, and that "some men and angels are predestined unto everlasting life, and others foreordained to everlasting death." Varying interpretations of this document have for over three centuries been the cause of disagreements, schisms, and the establishment of new denominations. It was such a disagreement in which William Tennent was embroiled as he proclaimed the Word of God in a pietistic manner that was

April. 29. 1647.

ORdered by the COMMONS *Assembled in Parliament, That* sixe *hundred Copies and no more of the* Advice of the Assembly of Divines, *Concerning a* Confession of Faith, with the Quotations and Texts of Scripture annexed, *presented to this House, and likewise* sixe hundred Copies *of the* Proceedings of the Assembly of Divines upon the thirty nine Articles of the Church of *England, be forthwith printed for the service of both Houses and the Assembly of Divines; And the Printer is enjoyned at his perill not to print more then* sixe hundred Copies *of each, or to divulge or publish any of them. It is further Ordered, that no Person presume to reprint, divulge, or publish the* said Advice, *or* Proceedings, *or any part of them till further order be taken by both or either of the Houses of Parliament.*

H. Elsynge Cler.
Parl. D. Com.

The humble

ADVICE

OF THE

ASSEMBLY

OF

Divines,

Now by Authority of PARLIAMENT sitting at *Westminster,*

Concerning a *Confession of Faith,* with the Quotations and Texts of Scripture annexed. Presented by them lately to both Houses of PARLIAMENT.

A certain number of Copies are Ordered to be Printed only for the use of the Members of both Houses and of the Assembly of Divines, to the end that they may advise thereupon.

LONDON,
Printed for the Company of STATIONERS.

Confession of Faith

Title page from the initial draft in 1647 reproduced from a copy in the Scheide Library through the courtesy of William H. Scheide, an emeritus trustee of the Seminary

uncongenial to the Old Side Presbyterians, most of whom were Scots-Irish and who emphasized a literal interpretation of the Bible and precise adherence to the Westminster Confession.

In the early eighteenth century the Scots-Irish "came in the thousands, bringing with them a belligerent brand of hard-shell Presbyterianism that accounts for the strong conservative tradition in the American church; . . . their enthusiasm and energy blended love of freedom and religious zeal that set its mark on these provinces." (Drummond, p. 45) Their attitude may be summarized by the prayer—"Grant, Lord, that I may be right, for Thou knowest that I am hard to turn."

8

Although widely scattered throughout the colonies during the early part of the eighteenth century there were sufficient Presbyterians in the Philadelphia area for a group of ministers in 1706 to establish the first American presbytery with the churches in that region as members. A decade later presbyteries had been organized in Philadelphia, Long Island, and Newcastle, Delaware. With a total church membership of more than three thousand distributed among some forty or more congregations it was possible for the three presbyteries to create the first synod on American soil. Not until 1789 were civil political conditions conducive and sufficient compromises possible for the creation of a General Assembly for all of the Presbyterian Church in the United States of America.

In contrast to Scotland, where the governance of the Presbyterian churches was established by the Scottish Parliament, the governmental structure of its counterpart in North America evolved from the congregations to the presbyteries, to the synods and eventually to the General Assembly. This hierarchical form of governance, which the Calvinists claimed was the true form of church government in the early Christian era, served as the main issue of disagreement with the Congregationalists of New England who believed in the autonomy of each local church. Whereas the Congregationalists, also adherents of Calvinism, assigned to each congregation responsibility to select and ordain its own minister, the Presbyterians assigned to the presbyteries authority to ordain ministers who might serve the Presbyterian Church universal. These two forms of government represented a basic distinction from the episcopal control of the Roman Catholic Church and its derivatives, the Church of England and the Protestant Episcopal Church in the United States.

Throughout history all religions and all denominations have encountered theological differences that have in many instances involved debates, altercations and even schisms. When the differences of conviction become intense the issue of religious control emerges and stimulates many forms of political maneuvering. The history of Presbyterianism in North America is only one example of this human phenomenon.

In every denomination religious control involves supervision of the selection, training, and ordination of future ministers who are committed to proclaiming the "true" path to eternal salvation. Such theological and religious debates among the Presbyterians in the middle of the eighteenth century led to the establishment of the College of New Jersey as the seat of learning for future New Side Presbyterian ministers, at a time when the only other colleges were Harvard, Yale and William and Mary. None of these institutions was then sympathetic to religious pietism.

College of New Jersey

Pietism has been described as

an effort to intensify Christian piety and purity of life. At the outset it also involved a protest against intellectualism, churchly formalism and ethical passivity. . . . Pietism was thus a movement of revival, aimed at making man's relation to God experientially and morally meaningful as well as socially relevant. It stressed the feelings of the heart. It emphasized the royal priesthood and sought to revive the laity. It called always for a return to the Bible. (Ahlstrom, p. 236)

The pietistic movement during the Great Awakening of the eighteenth century was led by such historic figures as Theodore Jacob Frelinghuysen, Jonathan Edwards, and George Whitefield. They recognized that for Christianity to fulfill its promises the church should complement its commitment to a creed with concern for the individual's way of life and personal conduct. Sympathetic to and active in the theological approach of these men were Gilbert Tennent and his brothers, Charles, John and William, each ordained sons of William Tennent. Joining them were Samuel Blair and Samuel Finley, former students at the Log College, as well as Aaron Burr, Sr. and Jonathan Dickinson, both graduates of Yale. They and others strongly supported the need for a college to educate future ministers for the propagation of New Side theology with its greater emphasis on evangelism. It was these men who established the College of New Jersey in 1746, first in the home of the Reverend Jonathan

Dickinson in Elizabeth, and on his death in the home of the Reverend Aaron Burr in Newark. In 1756 the college was moved to Nassau Hall in Princeton, the largest building in the colonies at that time and the domicile of the first students to enroll in Princeton Theological Seminary a half century later.

In the eighteenth century it was expected that Presbyterian ministers would be well educated, normally graduates of colleges before they underwent their apprentice training in the home of an ordained clergyman and before they assumed their ministry. Until additional colleges were founded in the colonies this requirement tended to limit ordination in the Presbyterian Church to men who were graduates of Harvard or Yale, or alternatively to those who were educated in Ireland or Scotland and emigrated to the colonies, or to the few native sons who could afford to pursue collegiate studies abroad. To provide for a succession of clergy the Congregationalists, Episcopalians, and Presbyterians, the three dominant denominations in the colonies in the eighteenth century, supported the establishment of colleges. This policy they pursued well into the nineteenth century by which time they were joined by almost all the other denominations in this ambitious educational enterprise.

Upon graduation from college the ministerial candidate would reside with a minister as a member of his family. During his period of residency of some months he would pursue assigned readings, write papers analyzing various Biblical topics, engage in theological discussions with his ministerial host, occasionally deliver a sermon, and accompany the minister on the daily visits to his various parishioners. At the conclusion of this tutorial the ministerial candidate would be examined by the presbytery as to his theological reliability and knowledge, and his suitability for ordination.

The establishment of the College of New Jersey assured a relatively rapid increase in the supply of New Side ministers, from twenty-two to seventy-three during the schism of 1741–1758. (Ahlstrom, p. 273) From the first twenty-one classes to be graduated from the College, 158, or forty-seven percent, entered the ministry, most of whom were New Side Presbyterians. During this period the struggle for control of the College, which ensued between New Side and Old Side adherents, was resolved in 1768 with the election to the presidency of John Witherspoon, a theologically moderate Scotsman whose political and religious influence was felt throughout the colonies soon after his arrival. He believed that both learning and piety were desirable characteristics for every Christian.

During Witherspoon's administration of twenty-six years, however, only twenty-four percent of the graduates entered the ministry, and the majority of them were members of the six classes immediately prior to the commencement of the Revolutionary War in 1776. Nevertheless, at the organization of the General Assembly in 1789, fifty-two of the 188 ministers had been pupils of Witherspoon, and eleven percent of the ministerial graduates either founded or were presidents of new colleges. Of political importance at this crucial time of national independence, Witherspoon was responsible for the education of six members of the Continental Congress, twenty-one United States Senators, thirty-nine Congressmen, ten cabinet officers, and twelve state governors. (Osgood, p. 12)

Although the College of New Jersey would continue to educate future ministers throughout the nineteenth century and although during this period the College would be dominated by ministerial control, the General Assembly of the Presbyterian Church decided in the early 1800s to follow the precedent of the Dutch Reformed and the Congregationalists and establish a seminary over which it would have direct control and which would ensure proper theological training of its future pastors. In 1784 the Dutch Reformed had established the New Brunswick Theological Seminary, and in 1808 the Congregationalists had organized Andover Theological Seminary.

A New Nation

The years that extended between the two wars with Great Britain—the American Revolution and the War of 1812—constituted an unsettling period for the citizens of this new nation. The population was expanding in both numbers and geography. Scots-Irish Presbyterians and others were emigrating to the middle colonies and then migrating farther westward from Pennsylvania and Virginia to Kentucky, Tennessee and elsewhere. Issues of commerce, war, civil government and law absorbed the active attention of the populace, not religion. Probably less than fifteen percent of this migrating and growing population was churchgoers. Despite these factors staunch Presbyterians exerted more influence on the development of the nation than at any other time in the history of the United States. By 1800 there were some four hundred congregations and twenty-six presbyteries.

More than twenty-one percent of the signers of the Declaration of Independence were Presbyterians, and the delegate to the Constitutional Convention, who has been attributed the greatest credit for the United States Constitution—James Madison—was a student of John Witherspoon. It may be noted that in broad terms the principles of the Constitution of the United States include many features that are similar to the Presbyterian form of governance. Among these features is the principle that was congruent with the teachings of John Calvin; namely, the principle of separation of church and state.

This was an era in the late eighteenth century when the Congregationalists in New England and the Presbyterians in the middle states provided the most influential religious force in this new nation. They were soon challenged, however, primarily by the Baptists and Methodists, as well as by some fundamentalist sects, and several decades later by Roman Catholics who immigrated in ever larger numbers from Germany, Ireland, Italy and other European countries.

In 1790 the nation's first census reported that ninety-four percent of the nation's four million population was located in the original thirteen states, a proportion that soon began to change as the appeal of western lands became irresistible for thousands of venturesome souls. It was the salvation of these souls that in part stimulated an increase in the demand for ministers in the various denominations. In the religious competition that ensued, as the nation expanded to the westward, the dominant denominations at the time of the Revolution lost their pre-eminent position. The Congregationalists and Presbyterians were especially vulnerable in this religious contest.

In contrast to the Baptists and Methodists who relied to a great extent on itinerant preachers, or circuit riders with limited formal education, the Presbyterians continued to insist on relatively thorough learning before ordination. Once ordained the Presbyterian minister had to be called by a local church, and on the frontiers congregations had to be formed before a minister could be called. Furthermore, the convictions of the Old School Presbyterians were strengthened at this time by the immigration of increasing numbers of Scots-Irish, many of whom were suspicious of any type of revivalism or deviations from the doctrines of the Westminster Confession of Faith, doctrines that were ill-adapted to frontier preaching. The Calvinistic aristocratic tenet of predestination had limited appeal for the self-reliant classless frontiersman.

During these years the traditional religions were also confronted with widespread theological skepticism and deism as proclaimed by Thomas Paine in his *Age of Reason* and practised by such national leaders as Benjamin Franklin and Thomas Jefferson. In this Age of Enlightenment skepticism was reinforced in the 1790s by the political and social upheaval in France following the revolution in that nation which had supported the American colonies in their struggle for independence.

Belatedly in 1801, in order to strengthen its position and influence, the General Assembly of the Presbyterian Church established with the Congregationalists of Connecticut a Plan of Union by which the two denominations would cooperate in establishing congregations, as well as colleges in the expanding settlements of the middle west. Although in time this joint enterprise became one of the issues that led to a schism among the Presbyterians in 1837, it did support the spread of Presbyterianism during the first third of the nineteenth century. It did not, however, appreciably increase the supply of ministers or the quality of their training and learning.

To address this need, as early as 1775 Jacob Green had proposed in a personal letter to a Congregational minister "a special two-year ministerial curriculum, bypassing the regular classical curriculum provided by the colleges," as a means of increasing the supply of qualified pastors. (Noll, *Journal of Presbyterian History*, p. 213) Green, a graduate of Harvard and one of the early trustees and officers of the College of New Jersey, had been influenced by the Great Awakening of the eighteenth century and was committed "to evangelizing the unreached and unruly segments of the expanding American frontier." (*ibid*) Although there was no immediate implementation of the Reverend Jacob Green's proposal by the Presbyterians, the Dutch Reformed church did establish a small seminary in New Brunswick, New Jersey in 1784, the earliest in the United States, as a means of meeting the needs that Green had wished to address. Of even more significance is the fact that Jacob Green was the father of Ashbel Green, one of the three individuals who rose to prominence in the Presbyterian Church and who were primarily responsible for the founding of Princeton Theological Seminary in the midst of the Second Great Awakening.

2

Now These Are the Names

EXODUS

The Great Awakening that occurred during the first decades of the nineteenth century accentuated the need among members of the Presbyterian Church for a larger number of clergy to minister to both the expanding population in the recently settled territories of the midwest and the growing number of parishes in the original thirteen states. The evangelical and revivalistic activities of charismatic ministers of some denominations also stimulated concerns among staunch Presbyterians that education for its ministry should emphasize both vital piety and sound theological learning. For some the College of New Jersey in the post-Witherspoon era was suspect with its introduction of science and modern foreign languages into the curriculum at the expense of what was then considered to be the necessary components of a pre-ministerial course of study. Denominationally controlled seminaries devoted singly to the preparation of future ministers in a sound theological manner and in an atmosphere undistracted by the foibles of youth were considered to be the proper answer. Such seminaries were also likely to produce a more dependable supply of ministers.

The leaders in this movement for a Presbyterian seminary were three ordained clergymen of markedly different temperaments who complemented each other, first in the creation of Princeton Theological Seminary and then in its operations until the middle of the nineteenth century. To appreciate their contributions one should first know something of each of their personalities.

Ashbel Green, the eldest, attained a position of some eminence at an early age. Graduating from the College of New Jersey in 1783 he presented the valedictorian address in the presence of George Washington. By the early 1790s Green had been ordained, was elected a trustee of the College, served as Stated Clerk of the General Assembly from 1790 to 1803 and chaplain to the United States Congress from 1792 to 1800. He maintained these responsibilities at the same time that he fulfilled his ministerial functions at the Second Presbyterian Church, founded by Gilbert Tennent in Philadelphia, where he remained until 1812 when he was selected as president of his alma mater. That was the same year in which his efforts to found the Seminary were realized. Aware of the value of political action Green was an intelligent, energetic, dominant force in the Presbyterian Church for nearly sixty years.

Samuel Miller was born in Delaware, also as Ashbel Green, in a Presbyterian manse. Following education at home under his father's tutelage he entered and was graduated with honors from the University of Pennsylvania in 1789. Within two years Miller became associated with the Presbyterian churches in New York City. Here he became a colleague of some of the ablest and best known ministers of that period and circulated with parishioners of wealth and social distinction. To this atmosphere he was well suited with his bland, formal but attractive, considerate, graceful manner, and his quick intellect. He wrote intelligently and extensively, and rose to a position of prominence in the church, including election as Moderator of the General Assembly in 1806, a position which enhanced his influence in supporting the establishment of a Presbyterian seminary. The following year he became a trustee of the College of New Jersey, which position he retained until his death in 1850.

The third member of this trio was Archibald Alexander. Born into a profitable farming family in the western part of Virginia he was provided educational opportunities that included instruction by the Reverend William Graham, a former student of John Witherspoon and later president of what became Washington and Lee University. Influenced by the religious revival in 1788 Alexander decided on the ministry and for a time became a missionary preacher in the rural areas of Virginia before becoming the pastor of two churches in the southern part of the Commonwealth. In 1797 at a young age he assumed the presidency of Hampden-Sydney College, a position that he held until 1807 with the exception of one year during which time he traveled through New Jersey, New York and New England and thus became personally acquainted with the theological attitudes of the Congregationalists and Presbyterians of those regions of the country.

It was on this trip in 1801 that he stopped in Princeton at the time of the College's commencement, was invited to sit on the platform, witnessed the awarding of nine honorary degrees, and then observed the trustees hurriedly convening and deciding to award him the honorary degree of master of arts. This action was not recorded in the trustees' minutes until a hundred years later, long after the College had recognized him again, this time with the doctor of divinity degree in 1810, and long after he had served as a trustee of the College from 1824 to 1851.

The reputation of this preacher, who could discourse without notes in an ingratiating and learned manner, had extended to the Pine Street Presbyterian Church in Philadelphia where he was called as pastor in 1807, the same year in which he was elected Moderator of the General Assembly at the young age of thirty-five. In the latter position he preached at the annual assembly the following year and publicly proposed the establishment of seminaries "for the single purpose of educating youth for the ministry, in which the course of education from its commencement shall be directed to this object;" namely, "a regular and sufficient supply of well qualified ministers of the gospel."

These are the three men who, with the assistance of many others, were primarily responsible for the creation of Princeton Theological Seminary. In the process of accomplishing their goal, however, they had to employ oral and written persuasion, as well as cajolery, and even shrewd political maneuvering.

The Period of Conception

The written records reveal that in March 1805, early in the rapidly developing movement to found theological seminaries, Miller wrote to Green—"It appears to me, that we ought forth-

Archibald Alexander
Seminary professor, 1812-1851

Samuel Miller
Seminary professor, 1813-1850

Ashbel Green
Chairman of the Board of
Directors of the Seminary
1812-1848

with, either to establish a new theological school, in some central part of our bounds; or direct more of our attention to extend the plan and increase the energy of the Princeton establishment [namely; College of New Jersey]." (Loetscher, *Facing the Enlightenment . . .* , p. 109) Miller's concerns were not limited to the need for clergy to fill vacant pastorates and his dissatisfaction with the curriculum at Princeton College; he also was filled with a denominational zeal to propagate Presbyterian convictions. Independence from Britain had removed the previous restraints and stimulated a missionary enthusiasm among most of the denominations with its corollary ingredient of denominational competition.

When Alexander proposed to the General Assembly in 1808 the establishment of one or more Presbyterian seminaries he already had the support of two of the more influential clergy from two of the important presbyteries: New York and Philadelphia. He also knew that the Hanover Presbytery in Virginia from whence he had moved to Philadelphia had demonstrated over many years an active interest in theological education. Furthermore, in that same year of 1808 the establishment by the Congregationalists of Andover Theological Seminary in Massachusetts had forced the Presbyterians to recognize the need for some action on their own part. Thus, in retrospect it is not surprising that in only four years a Presbyterian seminary was established.

The process involved the appointment by the General Assembly of several committees in succession to study and issue reports. One committee under the chairmanship of Samuel Miller solicited presbyteries for their attitudes toward the establishment of one or two seminaries under the control of the General Assembly, or the establishment of a number of smaller seminaries under the supervision of synods. Although the replies provided no obvious consensus, Miller's report interpreted the responses in such manner as to favor his preference for one seminary. To placate concerns of possible usurpation of authority by a seminary the report explicitly referred to the presbyteries' responsibility to examine and ordain ministers. And for those fearful that piety would be submerged by emphasis on strict education the report stated explicitly that a seminary should be "a nursery of vital piety as well as sound theological learning." To advance the process further the appointment of a successor committee was authorized with the charge to prepare a plan for the creation of a Presbyterian seminary. To this committee were appointed seven individuals of whom Alexander, Green and Miller were members. Green, as chairman, assumed major responsibility for the plan that was adopted by the General Assembly in 1811.

College of New Jersey

Concurrent with these developments the College of New Jersey, a Presbyterian sponsored and related institution but with an independent board of trustees, was experiencing minor convulsions. Even though a smaller percentage of its alumni were entering the ministry than in its earlier years, nevertheless in the early 1800s nearly twenty percent of its graduates each year became ministers. In fact, a steady percentage of its alumni through the rest of the century continued to engage in some type of clerical activity. The reduced supply of ministerial candidates was, however, an issue of major concern to Alexander, Green and Miller. They also abhorred the liberalization that they saw emerging while the college was being administered by Samuel Stanhope Smith.

Smith, the son of a Presbyterian minister who was a trustee of the College, as was Smith's maternal grandfather, was graduated with highest honors in 1769. Shortly thereafter he became a tutor at the College before serving as the first head of what later became Hampden-Sydney College, the same institution with which Alexander was later associated. Subsequently, he was recalled in 1779 to Princeton as professor of moral philosophy. His family associations with the College, strengthened by his marriage to the eldest daughter of John Witherspoon and by his own personal qualities, made him an ideal vice president to administer Princeton College, as it was colloquially known, during the period of recovery following the Revolutionary War years. Much of that time President Witherspoon was absent pursuing his national political and religious responsibilities. In 1795, following Witherspoon's death, Smith was elected president and began what was anticipated to be an auspicious administration but which ended sadly with his forced resignation in 1812, a resignation in which the primary advocates for a Presbyterian theological seminary were intimately involved.

In 1802 much of Nassau Hall was destroyed by a disastrous fire that some critics of the College claimed was set by unruly students. Although sufficient funds were soon raised to meet the costs of both repairing the damage and constructing two new buildings, one of which many years later was named Stanhope Hall, and although the enrollment had more than doubled in ten years, Smith was being criticized by Green, Miller and other conservative Presbyterian clerics. In 1807 a riot occurred that led to the suspension of over one hundred students with adverse reactions from the trustees, including both Green and Miller, as well as six new trustees whose confidence Smith did not enjoy. In 1807 for one reason or another six of the trustees had left the board. Two-thirds of their replacements and four continuing members of the board were later among the individuals appointed to serve on the first Board of Directors of the Seminary when it was organized in 1812. In view of these developments one may wonder where their primary loyalties lay during the discussions that ensued between the representatives of the College and the advocates for the Seminary.

With discussions for a seminary advancing relatively rapidly Smith and members of his board had been developing proposals that would have committed the College more intently to the education of ministerial candidates. In 1803 a professor of theology had been appointed to the faculty of the College to provide specialized instruction to ministerial candidates, but he had so few students that after three years he resigned. Other possibilities were pursued, and by the latter part of the decade, at a time when Smith's support was being eroded, he and a group of trustees, fearing for the future of the College, devised a proposal that they submitted to the General Assembly in 1811. This proposal would in effect have made the undergraduate academic activities of the College subordinate to the proposed theological program in most every respect. One insurmountable obstacle was the independent status of the Board of Trustees of the College that could not be made legally accountable to the General Assembly. A second obstacle was the spreading lack of confidence in the College, its president, its curricular tendencies and its disciplinary practices.

Another proposal, which contained potential adverse implications for the College and which never came to fruition, was the recommendation of the special committee of the General Assembly that an academy be established in conjunction with the proposed seminary for the purpose of preparing students for the theological course. Possible opposition from the College may have been the factor that prevented this provision from being implemented.

Smith was a clergyman of broad learning with an open mind in a denomination whose leaders at the time valued singleness of theological conviction to be a virtue. His cosmopolitan interests and his comments, for example, about anthropological and sociological issues raised doubts as to his religious integrity, and his customarily impeccable sartorial attire made him appear incongruous in the midst of clerical sameness.

Not only was the proposal that was presented by the College of New Jersey rejected in 1811 by the General Assembly but the following year, through maneuverings led by Samuel Miller, Smith was forced to resign. His severe critic, Ashbel Green, was immediately elected as the successor. Having harshly criticized Smith for his manner of handling student discipline Green's ten year administration proved to be no improvement.

This was a period of social unrest following the revolutions in North America and France, an era when the population of the United States was doubling in size and, following the Louisiana purchase, the geography of the young nation expanding several fold. It was the age of canal building and the dawn of the extensive railroad construction that extended through the nineteenth century. It was also the time of the second Great

Awakening during which the College experienced a student revival, much to Green's satisfaction.

This revival in 1815, which occurred undoubtedly with the encouragement of both Archibald Alexander and Samuel Miller, stimulated some forty Princeton College students to commit themselves to the ministry. It did not, however, prevent the continuation of student protests that partially accounted for Green's resignation as president in 1822. During the years that ensued, when at one time the enrollment dropped to only eighty students, the College encountered the lowest point in its history. Remaining under theological domination it continued to be a struggling institution until after the arrival from Scotland of James McCosh as president in 1868.

Plan of the Theological Seminary

The plan for the theological seminary presented by Ashbel Green and his committee was approved in its essentials by the General Assembly in 1811. It provided that the projected Theological Seminary of the Presbyterian Church in the United States of America shall be located between the Raritan and Potomac rivers and under the immediate control of a board of directors which, when organized in 1812, consisted of twenty-one ministers and nine elders. It assigned to the board authority to appoint and remove professors, to direct and examine the whole course of instruction, to direct the examination of students at least once each year, to watch over their conduct, and generally to superintend and endeavor to promote all the interests of the institution. The plan required the board to report annually to the General Assembly which retained the power of approval in such major issues as election of board members and appointment of members of the faculty. Among the stated purposes of the seminary were an increase in the supply of "enlightened, humble, zealous, laborious pastors to watch for the good of souls," the preservation and promotion of harmony and unity of the Presbyterian Church, and the founding of a nursery for missionaries to the heathen. This was the era when missionary movements were burgeoning with concerns for the eternal salvation of the heathen both at home and in other lands, as well as for the Afro-American peoples and the native American-Indians. Underlying the stated purposes was the intent to counteract what was perceived to be rampant religious infidelity in America by the education of a pious and learned ministry.

At this same assembly in 1811 it was reported that agents previously designated to solicit funds in each presbytery had already collected $14,000 for the proposed seminary. To advance the plans further Archibald Alexander was appointed chairman of a committee to meet with representatives of the College of New Jersey to consider issues of mutual concern including the possibility of locating the Seminary in the same town as the College. From the ensuing deliberations an agreement was readily reached by which the Seminary gained many benefits and the College attracted to its environs an institution with which for a century it had many entwined personal relationships.

The agreement provided that as long as the Seminary remained in Princeton the College would refrain from appointing a professor of theology to its faculty. The College also agreed to grant to the Seminary accommodation in its buildings and the privilege of constructing on the college campus such edifices as the Seminary might require for its professors and students. This latter provision was never employed. On the other hand, the one provision, which has been continued on a reciprocal basis uninterruptedly ever since, provided for the use by the Seminary personnel of the College library facilities.

At the meeting of the General Assembly in 1812 final approval was granted for the creation of a theological seminary and to the temporary establishment of it in Princeton on the basis of the agreement with the College. Corollary to this agreement was the offer of four acres of land by Richard Stockton, a local patriarch and long time college trustee. Further actions included appointment of the Board of Directors and the selection of the Seminary's first professor.

An intimate relationship between the governing boards of the two institutions was immediately established. Of the thirty men appointed to the original Board of Directors of the Seminary fourteen were then or at one time trustees of the College, and many others were either its alumni or the recipients of honorary degrees. Furthermore, six of the seven most recent moderators of the General Assembly were among the original directors.

The first meeting of the Board was held on June 30,1812, the same month in which the second war between the United States and Great Britain was declared. At that meeting Ashbel Green was elected president of the board, a position that he retained until his death in 1848—a period of thirty-six years. For various reasons in the following year of 1813 four men resigned from the board and were succeeded by individuals who included three additional trustees of the College. One of these was the wealthy Robert Lenox, who was a generous benefactor of both institutions, as was his son James throughout most of the nineteenth century.

The plan for the Seminary at Princeton, whose permanent location was determined in 1813, was predicated on the understanding that there would eventually be a minimum of three professors to teach courses in divinity, Oriental and Biblical literature, and ecclesiastical history and church government. The first professor chosen was Archibald Alexander, a learned and scholarly man whose indelible influence permeated the institution for generations.

Alexander's installation on August 12, 1812 signified the official establishment of the Theological Seminary of the Presbyterian Church in the United States of America, generally considered to be the first seminary in the western hemisphere to be organized by this denomination. Although it possessed no physical facilities, had only tenuous financial support, had enrolled merely three students, and appointed a single professor, Princeton Theological Seminary was as of that date a functioning institution.

3

These Be the Words

DEUTERONOMY

When the General Assembly of the Presbyterian Church had authorized the establishment of a seminary, and had selected the membership for the seminary's first Board of Directors, and had appointed its first professor, it became necessary to make provision to house this professor and to provide facilities for the housing and instruction of the anticipated students. To accomplish the latter responsibility the College of New Jersey (renamed Princeton University in 1896) had earlier agreed to provide space in its building, now known as Nassau Hall. For the Seminary's first professor, Archibald Alexander, a small house in Princeton was leased where he and his family could reside and where in a small study he could meet his students and shelve the incipient seminary library. (Many years later this privately owned house was moved from its site on the property now owned by Trinity Episcopal Church to 134 Mercer Street.)

After these arrangements had been made the Seminary of the Presbyterian Church in the United States of America opened in August of 1812 with three students. By the spring of 1813, the student body had increased to nine, a number that placed a heavier burden on the single professor and began to strain the facilities available in Nassau Hall. In response to these pressures Samuel Miller was appointed in 1813 to be the second professor in the Seminary, for which a permanent home in Princeton had now been endorsed, and the following year the General Assembly adopted the bold resolution of acquiring more property and of starting construction of a building of its own. Princeton Theological Seminary was now launched on a course that would throughout the nineteenth and twentieth centuries leave an indelible influence on Reformed theology and the life of the Presbyterian Church.

For more than three decades the words of two seminary professors, Archibald Alexander and Samuel Miller, each of whom lived until the middle of the nineteenth century, directly and indirectly affected the theological thoughts and reflections of hundreds of clergy and thousands of lay persons in both the Presbyterian and other Reformed denominations. Their words established the basis for the prestige that Princeton Theological Seminary attained in its first century of existence and has subsequently maintained throughout its second century despite the strains that occurred in the 1920s.

The following account of the Seminary that was established in Princeton one hundred and eighty years ago provides one view of a multi-faceted American religious history.

Early Years

During its early years and despite the distractions caused by the War of 1812 with Britain the enrollment of this fledgling institution increased steadily and by 1828 was over one hundred. For the next quarter of a century the average yearly enrollment was 126, fluctuating between 94 and 159. To accommodate this student body during the first half dozen years rooms and meals were made available by the College of New Jersey at an individual charge initially of $1.00 per week for room and board. It was also in Nassau Hall where the seminary lectures and recitations were held, and where the religious services were attended by students of both institutions in the presence of faculty members and their wives.

Within only two years of its founding the enrollment of the Seminary expanded beyond the capacity of the facilities available at the College so that about one-half of the seminary students were required to reside in lodgings in town. This fact and concern for the financial ability of students to meet their expenses, which amounted to a total of about $150 per year, caused the Board of Directors to recommend to the General Assembly the construction of a building that would provide for all the educational, religious, dining, and housing needs of the theological students. In 1815 the General Assembly made $15,000 available for this proposed building which became known as Old Seminary and which, when completed several years later, cost over $47,000.

The plans for the building, which were similar to Nassau Hall, were drawn by John McComb, Jr., the architect of such buildings as the current City Hall of New York. He was paid $100 for them and $5.00 for each day when he came from New York for inspection. The hours for the workmen, whose pay ranged between $1.50 and $2.00 per day, extended from sunrise to sunset on week-days, and from six in the morning to sunset on Saturdays invigorated with a daily supplement of "one gill and a half of ardent spirits."

Also in 1815 title to the four acres offered three years earlier by Richard Stockton was transferred to representatives of the Seminary and negotiations were concluded for the acquisition, partially by purchase, of seven more acres. At this same time a permanent home for Archibald Alexander was being planned and, after delays because of lack of funds, was constructed immediately to the east of Old Seminary. Here he moved at the end of the decade, two years before the kitchen was completed, and here he resided through the rest of his long, productive life.

Shortly after his move to Princeton in 1813 Samuel Miller built his own home on property that had belonged at the time of the Revolution to his father-in-law, Jonathan Dickinson Sergeant, a member of the Continental Congress and the first Attorney General of the Commonwealth of Pennsylvania. Through the remainder of their lives Miller and his wife occupied this property which is only a block from the Seminary and which now houses the Nassau Club.

While these buildings were being constructed and while scarce funds had to be collected to pay the salaries of the professors and provide financial assistance to students, none of whom was charged tuition, a course of study had to be developed and regular instruction conducted. Although the course of study was predicated on a three year program some students enrolled for only one or two years and entered at either one of two times during the year. The academic calendar provided two semesters: one from November to May, and the other from July to October. Under these conditions a heavy burden rested on the shoulders of Alexander and Miller.

The curriculum that they devised reflected a commitment to the divine revelation contained in the Bible, to the infallibility of the Holy Scriptures as the word of God, and to the doctrines of Calvinism. Week-day classroom lectures and recitations were supplemented by Sunday afternoon discussion sessions for faculty and students; these Alexander initiated shortly after the Seminary was established and were continued for many years after his death, well into the next century. He also created the Theological Society for which there were eight organizers, including five students. The purpose of their meetings, which were held twice a week, was mutual improvement in theological and kindred subjects.

The students themselves were energetic and purposeful in organizing groups to meet their collective religious goals, such as the Society for Improvement in the Composition and Delivery of Sermons, and the Society for Improvement in Biblical Literature, each of which met weekly. The creation by twenty seminary students of an additional organization in 1814, the Society of Inquiry Respecting Missions, was stimulated by growing support among both clergy and lay persons of most denominations for missionary activities. Their support was based on a commitment to improvement in human welfare and a conviction that individual salvation depended on commitment to Christianity. This was an era when voluntary benevolent national societies were being organized outside the structure of a single denomination, a development that would later contribute to a schism in the Presbyterian Church. Not only missions but issues relating to education, Sunday schools, recolonization, temperance and the distribution of Bibles and tracts had their separate local and national organizations.

Consistent with the spirit of these national organizations the Society of Inquiry Respecting Missions was organized to collect missionary intelligence from all quarters, to promote a spirit of missions, and to organize missionary activities for its members among local Afro-Americans and laborers, as well as to supply Sabbath school teachers for nearby churches. Through the activities of its sub-committees it conducted over a period of years extensive correspondence and stimulated a high percentage of Princeton Seminary graduates in the nineteenth century to enter the missionary field. The first from Princeton was Henry Woodward, who was in the class of 1818 and who devoted his life to missionary activities in India.

Another remarkable missionary of that period was Betsey Stockton, not a seminary student but taught to read by seminary students. She was the former slave of Elizabeth Stockton, the deceased and first of three wives of Ashbel Green. It was he who on Betsey's behalf overcame opposition to her becoming a missionary. Accompanying Charles S. Stewart '21 and his wife, who were going as missionaries to the Sandwich Islands (Hawaii) in 1822, Betsey Stockton remained there for several years during which time she started a school. Later she returned to Princeton where she was one of the founders of the Witherspoon Street Presbyterian Church and became active in the education of local Afro-American children.

As has been the pattern of Princeton Theological Seminary throughout most of its history its first ten years produced a group of influential alumni. Of the 256 graduates of that decade six were elected moderators of the General Assembly, two were consecrated bishops of the Protestant Episcopal Church, twenty-five were appointed professors and fifteen selected as presidents of colleges, including Pennsylvania, Yale and the College of New Jersey. Others became pastors of churches throughout the expanding nation, and some devoted their efforts to religious publications.

Board of Trustees

When land was actually acquired in 1815 and when the first building was completed a few years later, title to the property had to be assigned to three individuals since there was at that time no local incorporated body legally qualified to accept such assignment. By 1821, although funds were in short supply and sometimes insufficient to pay the professors' salaries, the permanent funds from which only interest could be used amounted to some $18,000. At the same time bequests were being received, scholarships and fellowships established, and yearly operating costs had increased to $4,500. In recognition of these developments the General Assembly adopted a resolution recommending that the Seminary be incorporated with a Board of Trustees to consist of twenty-one members, twelve of whom would be laymen. Such an act was approved by the New Jersey State Legislature in 1823. Thus, two boards shared responsibility in directing the affairs of the Seminary at Princeton for more than a century before this dual headed arrangement was at a time of considerable disruption discontinued in favor of a single governing board.

In essence, the original Board of Trustees, which held its first meeting in 1826, was responsible for fiscal affairs and physical property, and the Board of Directors continued to exercise supervision over academic, faculty and student affairs. In exercising their responsibilities the directors had codified an extensive list of regulations based on the requirement that "the [General] Assembly shall . . . ultimately sanction all its laws, direct its instructions, and appoint its principal officers."

The regulations included the following requirements selected for inclusion in this narrative because of their special interest to later generations.

The Board shall direct the Professors of the Seminary, in regard to the subjects and topics on which they are severally to give instruction to the pupils. . .

The Board of Directors shall inspect the fidelity of the Professors, especially in regard to the doctrines actually taught. . .

There shall be an examination of all pupils in the Seminary, at every stated meeting of the Board of Directors. . .

The hours of study and recreation for the students shall be fixed by the Professors, with the concurrence of the Directors. . .

Strict temperance in meat and drink is expected of every student, with cleanliness and neatness in his dress and habits, while all excessive expenses in clothing is strictly prohibited.

Of the some thirty Protestant seminaries that were in existence by 1840, six were Presbyterian of which Princeton was the largest. Records indicate that at Princeton in that earlier period daily schedules included rising bells at five followed by chapel, breakfast and then classes which extended from nine to noon. Following luncheon students were required to be studying in their rooms where they were subject to professorial inspections. All candles and oil lamps were to be extinguished by ten. Rooms were heated by wood burning fireplaces, and privies at the rear of Old Seminary provided the only toilet facilities. While there were no charges for room or tuition, students paid from $6 to $10 a year for wood, from $1.25 to $2.50 a week for meals, and paid separately for candles, laundry and other personal items. For students who resided in boarding houses expenses varied.

James Waddell Alexander '24 reported a somewhat different daily schedule since he rose at six and continued his studies until midnight at which time he "closed his eyes." Despite a busy schedule, or possibly because of it, his enthusiasm for life as a seminarian is apparent in his writing.

. . . we recite twice in three weeks on Hebrew, once on Greek, once on the Confession of Faith, once on Biblical History. Hear lectures once on Theology (preparatory to the full and regular theological lectures), twice on Biblical History, once on Criticism of the Original Scriptures, once on Jewish Antiquities. On Monday I attend a Society for the Improvement in the Criticism of the Bible. . . . On Tuesday night, the Theological Society, where every student delivers once in six weeks an original oration. On Thursday night, I am at liberty to attend evening lectures at the College. On Friday night, Theological Society, where questions in ethics and divinity are discussed. On Saturday night a weekly prayer meeting. On Sunday we have sermons from our three professors, and Professor [Philip] Lindsly [Vice President of the College of New Jersey] in rotation.

. . . we live in a kind of literary atmosphere; all the conversation carried on here is of a literary kind; at table, in our walks, and wherever a cluster of us assembles, some lively discussion takes place which causes our time to fly very rapidly and pleasantly away. (Alexander, *Forty Years . . . ,* p. 15–16)

From his report it is obvious that there was little time devoted to physical exercise, a condition that came to the attention of the directors when in 1829 a number of students became ill. Shortly thereafter a proposal was seriously considered, but rejected as being impractical, to adopt a work-study program at the Seminary in order that students would both derive benefit from physical exercise and income for their labors. Finances were an issue not only for students but also for the trustees who were faced with the responsibility of finding sufficient funds to pay operating expenses, faculty salaries, both often in arrears, and the costs of constructing additional facilities that the directors were proposing.

Buildings

Even after the construction of Old Seminary had been completed Sunday worship service continued to be held jointly with the College in Nassau Hall until 1826. In that year the Seminary began to hold its own independent services in the Oratory, a room created for that purpose in its new building, the same room in Alexander Hall that is still used by students for informal prayer sessions and other group meetings 170 years later.

Finding this space insufficient for the growing student enrollment the Board of Directors acted on a proposal of the professors and recommended in 1829 the erection of "a building to contain a chapel, a library and recitation rooms, as soon as funds can be obtained. . . ." In retrospect this action seems courageous when in the same decade the board was forced to address the problem of students enrolling for shorter periods of time than the expected three year course, when directors had to be reminded repeatedly to attend the examining sessions of students, and when many students did not bother to subject themselves to these examinations. In the social conditions of the pre-Civil War period the directors were also courageous when Theodore Wright '28, the first Afro-American to be graduated from the Princeton Seminary, was recommended by the Pres-

View of the Seminary Campus
1843

bytery of Albany for admission. By unequivocally declaring
that "his color shall form no obstacle in the way of his reception" the Board established a policy that has been maintained
ever since.

The aspirations of the Board of Directors were also shared by
the members of the Board of Trustees and the General Assembly since these two bodies endorsed the recommendation to
provide additional facilities "as soon as funds can be obtained."
By 1834 a new building, since 1893 identified as Miller Chapel
in honor of Samuel Miller, the second professor, was constructed to specifications designed by Charles Steadman, the
well-known local builder-architect, at a cost of some $6,000.
These funds were raised through appeals to various presbyteries under the coordination of Professor Charles Hodge. In 1824
Hodge had engaged the architect, John Haviland, to design his

35

own home which he had constructed at the west end of Old Seminary with the understanding that at a future date he would be repaid by the trustees for this building. The new chapel originally facing Mercer Street was located behind Old Seminary and the Alexander house. A companion building to house the library was to have been built, but never was, in a comparable position at the other end of and behind Old Seminary in a configuration similar to the location of the Clio and Whig Halls behind Nassau Hall on the College campus.

Even while the Seminary was dedicating a new building and entertaining plans for further physical expansion it was encountering difficulties in meeting its current operating expenses. Professors' salaries were in arrears, one scholarship fund was defunct because of a bank robbery, and other funds were strained because of the financial recession that occurred in the country during the populist administration (1829–1837) of President Andrew Jackson, who had continually attacked the national banking system. To solicit funds during these difficult times the Seminary engaged special agents, including two seminary graduates in the classes of 1822 and 1833 respectively. John Breckenridge served in this capacity in 1835 and Cortland van Rensselaer served from 1843 to 1845 during which period the latter raised approximately $100,000 for which he accepted no remuneration.

Before Breckenridge's appointment a large number of alumni at the meeting of the General Assembly in 1833 decided to form an association whose objectives would be to renew and perpetuate the friendships and associations which subsisted among them when fellow-students, to promote personal piety, to foster the spirit of missions, to incite greater diligence in the work of the ministry, and to support the beloved institution in which they received their theological education, in so far as their influence can be auxiliary to this worthy cause. It was through the commitment and influence of these clergy and others that lay persons increased their support for the Seminary.

One of the exceptionally munificent individuals was James Lenox, the son of Robert Lenox, a wealthy Scot from New York who became interested in the Seminary when he first served as a director in 1813 and later as a trustee. His son James, who retired from business at an early age, succeeded his father as a trustee in 1831, a position he held until a year before his death in 1880. Although the name of Lenox is still well known as a result of his and his family's many benefactions in the City of New York, he was generous both to Princeton College and to Princeton Seminary, especially the latter.

His first major gift to the Seminary included a house on the site where Erdman Hall now stands and approximately five acres of land on which he constructed a library building. This property and the buildings, which were valued at $32,000 in 1843 when he deeded them to the Seminary, were not located behind Old Seminary as earlier plans for a library had projected, but across Mercer Street adjacent to Steadman Street, later renamed Library Place. Although within a few years the library building housed a collection of over 9,000 volumes, as was the custom in most collegiate institutions of those days it was open for use only a limited number of hours each weekday. Lack of illumination and fear of fires were contributing factors, as well as need for adequate library personnel.

Only a few years after the opening of the Lenox Library the Seminary was again encountering serious difficulty in meeting current expenses even though in 1844 the permanent funds amounted to $99,500 of which $60,700 was designated for professorships and $38,800 for scholarships. In recognition of the need for funds to assist with general operating costs, several men of wealth in New York in 1846 raised $7,500 to start an endowment the income from which would be designated for current expenses.

Despite these financial concerns, in that same year plans were announced for the construction of a refectory with kitchen and dining facilities intended to provide nourishing meals at reasonable costs. This building may have been partially stimulated by complaints expressed earlier in a petition submitted by a number of students that resulted in the dismissal of a steward. At a cost of some $8,000 the building, which also included housing accommodations for the steward and space for a small student infirmary, was completed in 1847. The building was designed

Lenox Library
Interior view after installation of electric lighting in the latter part of
the nineteenth century

by John Notman, the distinguished Philadelphia architect. Funds for the construction of this new building, which in 1945 was assigned to the use of the administration, were raised from a number of individuals, only ten years after the great schism of the nineteenth century that had bitterly split the Presbyterian Church in the United States of America and had led to legal contentions for control of the Seminary.

Doctrinal Differences

The theological convictions of many of the faculty, directors, and trustees, as well as a number of other supporters of Princeton Theological Seminary throughout the nineteenth and first decades of the twentieth century were explicitly represented in the deed of May 5, 1843 when James Lenox transferred title for his gift of the Lenox Library.

PROVIDED ALWAYS NEVERTHELESS and upon this condition that if at any time or times hereafter the said parties of the second part shall pass from under the supervision and control of the General Assembly of the Presbyterian Church in the United States of America now commonly known and distinguished as the Old School General Assembly and its successors, or if at any time or times hereafter the leading doctrines declared as the confession of faith, and catechisms of the Presbyterian Church, such as the doctrines of universal and total depravity, the doctrine of election, the doctrine of the atonement, the doctrines of the imputation of Adam's sin to all his posterity and of the imputation of Christ's righteousness to all his people for their justification, the doctrine of human inability and the doctrine of the necessity of the influence of the Holy Spirit in the regeneration, conversion, and sanctification of sinners, as these doctrines are now understood and explained by the aforesaid Old School General Assembly, then and in either case the Grant and Conveyance, hereby made, shall cease and BECOME NULL AND VOID . . .

Added to these strong doctrinal convictions on the part of ardent Presbyterians of the Old School was the irrevocable commitment to the constitution of their church. Its structure, not to be revised to meet any historical contingency, but only on the basis of the clear teaching of the Scripture, was an article of true faith. For those who subscribed to these doctrines and who believed that the Bible and the Confession of Faith were in full accord, the Plan of Union of 1801 with the Congregationalists of New England, had been both a theological and political error that should be renounced. Inter-denominational recognition of ordination and independent cooperative boards for missions and other joint religious activities, which this compact provided, undermined the ecclesiastical principles on which their Presbyterianism was based. These jointly supported activities also impeded denominational control and were contrary to the spirit of competition on which denominationalism thrived.

To appreciate the social environment that existed in the 1830s one must recall that the Jacksonian period was partially one of rebellion and a struggle for equality in a society augmented by cultural, ethnic and religious pluralism. The expanding west felt oppressed by the east and its banking structure. This period experienced the growth of the political spoils system, the emergence of science, a rapidly expanding railroad transportation system, the development of Transcendentalism and of Unitarianism, the influence of German scholars on Biblical analysis, and the intensifying conflict over slavery, a curse from which this nation has suffered throughout its history. Added to these traumatic forces that directly and indirectly affected Presbyterianism was the influx of thousands upon thousands of Irish and other immigrants who were nurtured in the Roman Catholic faith, who retained their denominational adherence, and who by so doing unwittingly presented a threat to those whose ancestors had fought against political and religious Catholic domination.

It was in this social and political climate that the adherents of Calvinism with their concerns for individual salvation became sufficiently numerous and politically strong to control the General Assembly of 1837 at which the Plan of Union of 1801 was renounced and several opposing synods in western New York and Ohio were expelled. This rupture, which the professors at Princeton Seminary only modestly discouraged, established its allegiance to Old School Presbyterianism. At the same time the schism hindered the church from fully addressing the opportunities available in a rapidly expanding nation, opportunities that other denominations recognized and on which they amply capitalized with their emphasis on what Lefferts A. Loetscher '28 professor at the Seminary from 1941 to 1974, called "spontaneity, vital impulse and adaptability." (Loetscher, *Broadening Church*, p. 1)

In times of flux and uncertainties human nature often becomes especially protective and tends to adhere to traditional thoughts and actions. Deviations among cohorts often lead to bitter struggles as was the case with the Presbyterians and their somewhat frequent heresy trials during the nineteenth century. Even the president of Lane Seminary in Cincinnati, Lyman Beecher, although ultimately exonerated, was subject to such a trial during the strains of the pre-Civil War years.

Princeton Theological Seminary was not immune to these influences. To decide the issue of its control a law suit was instituted as a result of which the Old School General Assembly maintained its authority of supervision. Despite these distractions the Seminary at Princeton continued to be the largest of the forty-five Protestant seminaries that were in existence in 1855, six of which were Old School and five New School Presbyterian. Its prestige rested not on the fact that it was officially the Seminary of the Presbyterian Church but on the reputation of its small faculty of outstanding theologians and teachers.

The Faculty

Every educational institution requires a faculty to teach, a student body to learn, a governing structure to administer, facilities in which to teach and learn, a library and equipment to assist in both teaching and learning, and sufficient financial support to make all this possible. From the inauguration of Archibald Alexander in 1812, as the first professor of the Seminary, to his death in 1851 there was constant need for increased financial support which Divine Providence, with the assistance of many committed individuals, seemed eventually to provide. Four major buildings were constructed. The student enrollment remained reasonably constant even during the period following the schism of 1837. The library holdings were continually being expanded. There was a modicum of administrative structure, since the senior member of the faculty was required to assume many of these responsibilities. The two governing bodies operated in tandem and harmony with the conservative policies of the General Assembly. While all of these factors contributed to the prestige of Princeton Theological Seminary, it was the quality of the faculty that was the primary ingredient of its reputation. Prior to 1850 only six men were appointed to professorships and two of these each served just two years.

Of the trio of individuals who were primarily responsible for the establishment of the seminary, Ashbel Green was the first to die—in May 1848. Although not a professor he did teach several years on a part-time basis during the period of his presidency of the College. Following his resignation from that position and return to Philadelphia in 1822 he continued a busy life of writing and preaching, and he maintained his position with the Seminary as president of its Board of Directors through his eighty-sixth year. Part of that time he was also a member of its Board of Trustees. The contributions of this Green family—there was another and distinct Green family anon—were enhanced by one of Ashbel Green's sons, James Sproat Green, a local lawyer of distinction, a United States District Attorney, and trustee of the College; he served in the important position of treasurer of the Seminary from 1818 to his death in 1862.

The second of the three primary founders of the seminary to die was Samuel Miller—in January 1850, a year and a half after he had retired in his 80th year. Having been called to serve parishes in New York in 1792 when there were less than two dozen ministers of various faiths in the city and less than two hundred Presbyterian ministers in all the states, he was immediately engrossed in the political issues of the new republic. Opposed to slavery, an advocate of the goals of the French Republic, active in the emerging missionary efforts, Miller was outspoken in his early years for various social causes. In time he tempered what he later considered to be his excesses but he never restrained his insistence on temperance and his denominational commitment to the Old School Presbyterian theology.

The influence that Miller had on his seminary students may be imagined from some of the phrases employed in describing his personality: gentle, generous, genial, elegant and courtly; full of conversation, rich in anecdote; calm and precise; logical and effective preacher; widely read and tenacious memory. A friend of his observed that "his mind was historical in tendency; his eloquence was singularly persuasive, and his literary acquisitions extensive." In 1953 Professor Gilbert Chinard of Princeton University noted that "one hundred and fifty years ago a young minister of the Presbyterian Church, the Reverend Samuel Miller, published in New York, under the title of *A Brief Retrospect of the Eighteenth Century*, a little-known work which might well be considered one of the earliest and most important contributions of an American to cultural history." (Chinard)

With his intellectual competence and his precise manner Miller was critical of the evangelistic approach to religion and for him the deplorable quality of Presbyterian worship. In *Thoughts on Public Prayer*, published in the year before his death, "he gave a depressing analysis of frequent faults of public 'free' prayer, such as infelicities and solecisms of language, lack of organization and the omission of important elements, wearisome length, empty rhetoric, didacticism."

This gentleman of the Old School, both in personality and theology, left an everlasting imprint on the Seminary and its students during the first half of the nineteenth century. As did Ashbel Green, Miller also had a relative who was closely involved in seminary activities—a son-in-law, John Breckenridge whose father had been a United States Senator from Kentucky and Attorney General in the administration of Thomas Jefferson. Having been secretary of the Presbyterian Board of Education, in which position he had forcefully and publicly attacked the Roman Catholics, the younger Breckenridge was appointed in 1835 to serve on the faculty and concurrently be the Seminary's agent to solicit funds. The first to teach a seminary course on missions, this enthusiastic, energetic and genial young man was soon enticed, however, to become the secretary of the denomination's Board of Foreign Missions just prior to the split of the church in 1837. Thus his tenure at the seminary was short lived.

The last of the early triumvirate and in many respects the most important was Archibald Alexander who died in 1851 in his seventy-ninth year. Alexander possessed sterling personal qualities that suited him admirably for the position of leadership in establishing the first Presbyterian seminary, and one of the first Protestant seminaries in the United States. A humble man of gentle nature with a wide ranging and inquiring mind, he was an ideal mentor for the hundreds of students whom he taught in his thirty-nine years as the senior professor in the Seminary.

Having established early in his life an interest in missions, an active interest which he shared with Samuel Miller throughout their lives, Alexander encouraged his students to enter the mission field. Within the first twenty-five years fifty students embarked for overseas assignments which required them to transport all their books and personal supplies, including even bed linen. Consuming as much as four months at sea to reach their destinations these long trips permitted the young ordained missionaries to practice their Sunday school teaching on the ship's crews. It was for some a dangerous endeavor on which they were embarked. The lives of Levi Janvier '40 and Walter M. Lowrie '41 ended in violent deaths; the former thrown overboard by pirates in the China Sea, and the latter stabbed by a Sikh in India. These and other similar incidents did not, however, discourage subsequent seminary graduates in proportionately large numbers to enter the overseas mission field.

Less successful were Alexander's efforts to encourage missionary work with the native Indians and especially the blacks. As a pastor both in Virginia and later in Philadelphia he had been actively involved in organizing churches for his black brethren and was as concerned for their individual salvation as he was for whites. Among the dozen or so Princeton seminarians, who for at least a short time served as missionaries to slaves, was Charles Colcock Jones. In 1830, the year in which he completed his studies at the Seminary, he organized the Society of Enquiry Concerning Africans and two years later became a full-time missionary to the slaves in his native south.

To some, Alexander's attitude toward slavery may seem ambiguous. He did not condone human bondage, an issue that was rending both the nation and the religious denominations; rather, he endeavored to remain neutral, placing his emphasis on saving individual souls, not on the economic and political structure under which the individuals lived. One may conjecture that his abhorrence of the accelerating pace of abolition may have been based on a desire to avoid social chaos, and his theological conservatism may have been reinforced by a desire to maintain cultural stability.

This conservatism, which was established by Alexander and Miller, was the hallmark of Princeton Theological Seminary for over a century. Alexander's contribution has within recent years been analyzed by many theological historians including Henry W. Bowden, professor of religion at Rutgers University. Writing in the foreword to Leffert A. Loetscher's volume on Alexander, Bowden commented—

Though Alexander was personally moderate and fair minded, he nevertheless fostered in his institution a static view of history that denied progressive change, a commitment to Biblical inerrancy, and a refusal to cooperate with either those caught in error or those who compromised denominational priorities. Princetonians claimed to be open to critical study, but they actually underscored timeless truths in their lectures, manifesting a non-historical approach that produced undeviating adherence to orthodox conclusions. (Loetscher, *Facing the Enlightenment* . . . , p. viii)

Whereas this analysis just quoted could have been applied to most theological seminaries and their faculties in much of the nineteenth century, a more personal observation by Mark Noll, professor of history at Wheaton College, Illinois, emphasizes the human qualities of Archibald Alexander that both his contemporaries and his students respected.

He published widely on theology, history, apologetics, moral philosophy, and religious experience, but his works are not so technical or so weighty as those of his successors. . . . Yet Alexander was the most winsome of the major Princeton professors. Testimonials concerning the moving power of his preaching, the effectiveness of his spiritual counsel, the relaxed demeanor of his family circle, and the relative latitude of his ecclesiastical views mark him as a forceful and engaging personality of nearly heroic proportions. (Noll, *Princeton Theology*, p. 13)

In common with many large families the Alexanders produced seven children of whom two of his three clerical sons were appointed to professorships in the seminary. In more recent times questions would be raised about possible nepotism with such sanguinolent relationships, but not in the case of the Alexanders, each of whom was exceptionally brilliant.

After graduating from the College of New Jersey in 1820 at the age of sixteen, James Waddell Alexander completed a course of study at the seminary in 1824, held pastorates in Virginia and Trenton, and then taught at the College for a decade before accepting the call from a congregation in New York. Enticed in 1849, near the end of his father's life, to a professorship at the Seminary, he remained only two years, unable to resist the appeal to return to his former parish in New York. While his professorial contributions at the Seminary were brief, this handsome, articulate preacher wrote over one hundred articles for the *Princeton Review*, the influential publication that for many decades enunciated the religious convictions of Princeton Theological Seminary.

The other professorial son, Joseph Addison Alexander, was considered to be "a whirlwind as a teacher and a preacher." He was also an infant prodigy, precocious, a brilliant linguist, knowledgeable in at least two dozen languages, many of which he learned by himself. He was graduated from the College of New Jersey in 1826 where he taught for several years after co-founding a local boys school; he then studied in Europe before accepting a professorship at the Seminary where he had begun teaching in 1836. Full of humor and kindness, sincere and pious, this younger Alexander son wrote incessantly and productively with a firm faith in the Bible until his early death at age fifty-one.

The sixth professor to be appointed prior to 1850, but the third in order of appointment, enjoyed a longer association with the Seminary than any other individual. It began when as a small boy he witnessed the inauguration of Archibald Alexander in 1812 and ended with his death in 1878. He taught theology to more students than any other professor at Princeton Seminary, and his writings were more widely read than almost any other Protestant theologian of the nineteenth century. Elected to the faculty in 1820 Charles Hodge became the individual with whom the Princeton theology became most singularly identified well into the early part of the twentieth century.

4

Blessed is the Man

PSALMS

With the deaths of Archibald Alexander and Samuel Miller an era in the history of Princeton Theological Seminary came to an end, but not an end to its theological convictions. No one adhered to them more assiduously than Charles Hodge and no one has been more intimately identified than he with the Reformed religious traditions for which the Seminary in Princeton was known well into the twentieth century.

The first words of the book of Psalms proclaim—

Blessed is the man that walketh not in the counsel of the ungodly, nor standeth in the way of the sinners, nor sitteth in the seat of the scornful.

But his delight is in the law of the Lord; and in his law doth he meditate day and night.

To no professor at the Seminary could these words apply more aptly than to Charles Hodge. Most of his long life was committed to the law of the Lord and an espousal of His law through teaching, sermons, and writings. During periods of illness and pain, as author and editor, he endlessly wrote: articles, commentaries, lectures, letters, and tracts, culminating late in life with his extensive three volume publication, *Systematic Theology*.

Born in Philadelphia in 1797, but fatherless at an early age, Hodge was brought to Princeton where his mother established her home. Here he entered the College of New Jersey from which he was graduated with a high scholastic record in 1815. Influenced by a religious revival that occurred on the campus at that time, he with eight other members of his class entered Princeton Seminary which course of study he completed in 1819. Among the many friendships that he developed in both

48

college and seminary none was closer than that which lasted a life-time with John Johns, later president of the College of William and Mary and Episcopal Bishop of Virginia.

After an additional year of reading and study Hodge was appointed tutor at the College by Ashbel Green, its president, who had known him as a small boy in Philadelphia. During the two years, 1820–1822, that Hodge served as tutor the burdens placed on Alexander and Miller by the increasing student enrollment at the Seminary convinced its Board of Directors to recommend approval by the General Assembly of the appointment of a third professor. With his intellectual competence and with Alexander his mentor, Hodge was the logical individual to receive this assignment even though he was only twenty-four years of age at the time. Thus began the longest and most remarkable tenure of any professor at Princeton Theological Seminary.

Within a few weeks of the inauguration of his seminary professorship Hodge was married to Sarah Bache, the great-granddaughter of Benjamin Franklin. It was her funds that helped to include some of the amenities still to be noted in the Hodge House; it was she who cared for students when ill; it was she who alone raised their son Archibald Alexander Hodge, born in July 1823, while her husband Charles spent two years studying in Europe with approval and encouragement of the Seminary directors.

In the early nineteenth century German academicians were developing philology, and the theologians were analyzing and interpreting Biblical texts along more informed critical lines. With his intellectual inquisitiveness and theological brilliance Hodge recognized the value of his direct exposure to these academic movements. His extended European sojourn included months of study in Paris, Halle, and Berlin followed by a brief tour of the British Isles. From this sabbatical experience, as his extensive writings would later attest, he seems to have been less impressed by the Biblical interpretations of German historiographers than by three other ideas: "the value of civil and religious liberty, the importance of religious instruction in the public schools, and the intimate connection between speculative opinion and moral character." (Salmond, p. 30)

Shortly after joining the Seminary faculty and before his European experience Hodge had initiated a journal in 1825 which he called the *Biblical Repertory*. Four years later, when there were already in existence some 170 religious publications in the United States, the name was changed to the *Biblical Repertory and Theological Review* and several times subsequently to other titles. Much later it was the *Princeton Review* by which it has historically been known. Regardless of the title, this publication provided Hodge as the principal editor with the means to comment publicly on every theological controversy, and this he did and thus he exerted a wide influence on broad religious and social issues, an influence that extended far beyond those of the Reformed faith. At the time Hodge was withdrawing as editor in the 1870s a British journal stated, "It is beyond all question the greatest purely theological review that has ever been published in the English tongue, and has waged war in defense of the Westminster standards for a period of forty years, with a polemic vigor and unity of design without any parallel in the history of religious journalism." (Thorp, p. 203)

Society in Flux

The peoples of every age consider that they are undergoing dynamic changes that are exceptional and that they are forced to confront a configuration of issues which have not previously existed. Those living in a later century cannot fully appreciate the concerns and worries of the men and women who were contemporaries of Charles Hodge. However, later generations can at least enumerate some of the dynamic social conditions that their ancestors faced in the nineteenth century, conditions that caused those who are now long deceased just as much anguish as any agonies encountered by those living more than a century later.

Hodge witnessed the geographical expansion of the country, accelerated by the construction of thousands of miles of railroad tracks. He saw a nation applying science and technology, solic-

BIBLICAL REPERTORY.

A

Collection of Tracts

IN

BIBLICAL LITERATURE.

BY CHARLES HODGE,

PROFESSOR OF ORIENTAL AND BIBLICAL LITERATURE, IN THE THEOLOGICAL
SEMINARY, AT PRINCETON, NEW JERSEY.

Ἐρευνᾶτε τὰς γραφας.

VOL. I.

Princeton Press:

PRINTED BY D. A. BORRENSTEIN.

1825.

Biblical Repertory
Title page of the first issue in 1825 of
Charles Hodge's publication

iting the investment of foreign capital, and employing foreign immigrants whose presence accelerated industrialization and urbanization. He experienced a demand for educated clergy to fill the growing number of church pulpits as well as missionary assignments during a period when many other denominations were expanding more rapidly than the Presbyterians. In his defense of Calvinism he withstood the threats, as he perceived them, of the emerging academic disciplines of anthropology, psychology, sociology, and the theory of evolution. All of these forces were disturbing to a man whose nature was "sunny, genial, kindly and tolerant" (Scott, W.B., p. 8), but they did not dissuade him from being throughout his lifetime an ardent advocate for the Word of God not only as the basis of human salvation but also as a stabilizing force for society. With his desire for peace and stability he was unable to face directly the one social force that engulfed the entire nation and nearly split it permanently asunder.

At first the issue of slavery was a nuisance, then a cause, finally a national issue that political compromise could not resolve. Denominational schisms and military conflict ensued. The Presbyterian Church had split in 1837 between the factions of the Old School and those of the New School partially over the issue of slavery. With the firing on Fort Sumter it was inevitable that the church would split further, between the south and the north as many denominations did, a division that was not healed among the Presbyterians until late in the twentieth century. On the other hand, the schism of 1837 was mended in 1869 when compromises were possible and the two separate bodies agreed to reunite. By this time, when the Old School faction was nearly twice as large in communicants as the New School, both groups needed each other as other denominations with their reliance on revivalism were expanding much more rapidly.

On each occasion, in 1837 and again in 1869, Hodge opposed the actions that were taken, in the second instance at least partially because of fear that the former advocates of the New School theology might be able to amend the Old School commitment to the Westminster Confession of Faith to which

Princeton Theological Seminary strongly adhered. Opposition to revivalism and excessive piety were also factors of importance. From its founding the Seminary looked askance at revivalism, an approach to religion that caused less concern to the New School advocates. Hodge and his colleagues were convinced that revivalism tended to stress numbers, to encourage individualistic and charismatic leadership, to be anti-intellectual, and to rely on emotional excesses with less attention to the principles that the Princeton Seminary stressed; namely, an intellectual approach to religion with emphasis on inward self-commitment and personal salvation.

In contrast to Hodge's fears the conservative theological influence of the Seminary remained strong, if not stronger, within the Presbyterian Church for a number of years following the reunion of 1869. Furthermore, as a consequence of the reunion some of the limitations that had been imposed by the General Assembly on the Seminary were amended to permit more freedom of action and independence on the part of its Board of Directors and its Board of Trustees. In contrast to the original provision by which appointments of professors and directors were subject to approval by the General Assembly the revisions in 1870 granted to the General Assembly the power only to veto such appointments during a period of one year after they were made. Despite this change and subsequent amendments to the charter of the seminary by which the Board of Trustees was enlarged, the personnel of the faculty and the two boards continued to be markedly cohesive, at least until the 1920s.

Faculty Personnel

When Hodge became senior professor on the death of Archibald Alexander there were three professors on the faculty of the seminary. Hodge had been appointed in 1822, Joseph Addison Alexander in 1838, and William Henry Green in 1851.

Despite many family associations with the College of New Jersey Green had enrolled at Lafayette College from which he was graduated at age sixteen. Upon completion of his studies at

Charles Hodge and Faculty Colleagues, 1873
Seated, left to right: Alexander T. McGill, Charles Hodge;
Standing: James C. Moffat, Caspar Wistar Hodge, Charles A. Aiken,
William Henry Green

the Seminary in 1846 he served as an instructor before his appointment to a professorship. For most of the history of the Seminary each professor was inaugurated at a special ceremony at which he was expected to deliver a sermon. In the first sentences of his inaugural discourse in 1851 Green indicated his theological commitment from which he never deviated.

The religious questions of the age seem to be concentrating more and more about one point—the authority due to the Holy Scriptures. Are they the sole infallible rule of faith? Or are they an infallible rule of

Faculty Members, 1888
Seated, left to right: James C. Moffat, Francis Landey Patton,
William Henry Green, William M. Paxton; *Standing*: Caspar Wistar
Hodge, Charles A. Aiken, Benjamin B. Warfield, John D. Davis

faith at all? It is here precisely that there must be fought the grand
battle with Ritualism on the one hand, and with Scepticism on the
other.

By the spring of the following year Green had submitted to
the members of the Board of Directors for their perusal an out-
line of the courses that he had been assigned to teach. So
pleased were the directors with this procedure that they adopted
the policy of requiring such submission from all professors in
the future.

Because of Green's wide reputation as an Old Testament scholar, his staunch theological conservatism, his long tenure, and his extensive family involvement in the affairs of both Princeton Seminary and Princeton College, it is pertinent to note that in 1868 he declined an official offer of the presidency of the College. Following this decision James McCosh, the venerable Scottish cleric, accepted the position in which he was able to reinvigorate the institution that had been largely dormant ever since the Seminary was founded in 1812. At the same time Green was elected to the Board of Trustees of the College and shortly thereafter chairman of the trustees' Committee on Library and Apparatus, positions that he held until his death.

Hodge's support for the traditional theological stance of the Seminary was reinforced first by Green, and then through the remainder of the nineteenth century by subsequent appointments to the faculty of men with similar convictions. With the exception of a few years the faculty had consisted of three professors until the early 1860s when it was increased to five and included the following departments: Old Testament, New Testament, church history, didactic theology, and practical theology, with the addition of ethics and apologetics in 1871. This first professorship of ethics in any seminary was stimulated by Stephen Colwell, a trustee from 1843 to 1871, who strongly criticized "the way in which churches in the nineteenth century have linked themselves to a burgeoning free enterprise economy, have supported an industrial revolution in society, but have been little concerned about anything but the most palliative relief for the victims of social change." (Bruce Morgan in Kerr, *Sons of Prophets*, p. 127)

Following William Henry Green's inauguration there were thirteen seminary professors appointed prior to 1900: in 1854 Alexander T. McGill, in 1860 Caspar Wistar Hodge '53, in 1861 James C. Moffat, in 1871 Charles A. Aiken, in 1877 Archibald Alexander Hodge '47, in 1880 Francis Landey Patton '65, in 1883 William Miller Paxton '48, in 1887 Benjamin Breckenridge Warfield '76, in 1888 John D. Davis '83, in 1892 John DeWitt '64, George T. Purves '76, and William Brenton Greene, Jr. '80, and in 1893 Geerhardus Vos '85. Of these thirteen professors all but three were alumni of the Seminary, seven had been students of Charles Hodge and two were his sons. Calvinistic doctrines as espoused at Princeton Seminary were inbred in their souls.

While each of these professors made significant contributions to the Seminary and its students, the one who was the torch bearer of Princeton theology was Benjamin B. Warfield. Born in Kentucky into a well-to-do family he was graduated from both Princeton College and Princeton Seminary, studied at Leipzig in Germany, and held several pastorates before teaching at Western Theological Seminary in Pittsburgh. From there he moved to Princeton as the successor to the younger Hodge who had previously succeeded his father, Charles Hodge. Warfield was an erudite, penetrating, precise scholar with wide ranging interests. Uninterested in the political interplay of church affairs but committed to the education of future Presbyterian ministers he taught and wrote prolifically with a resolute commitment to Biblical authority. Writing in the *Princeton Seminary Bulletin* in February 1965, Gwilym O. Griffith '09, a Welshman, described his recollections of Warfield.

With his noble head, his impressive profile, his patriarchal beard, he exhaled authority. Perhaps he was more impressive when sitting, for his stature was not commanding; but, gowned and seated at his lecture-desk, he inspired something akin to awe. His utterance was marked by a slight—very slight—lisp, which was by no means an impediment; oddly enough, it lent character and distinction to his speech.

Even after his death the dominant influence of this professor would continue to be a factor when the cataclysm of the late 1920s exploded on the campus of Princeton Seminary.

Trustee Personnel

As has been noted earlier there was during the nineteenth century much overlapping of board membership between the two major educational institutions in Princeton. This overlap included some faculty from each institution serving on the other institution's boards, and it involved many individuals serving on the boards of both institutions simultaneously. Of the twenty professors appointed to the Seminary faculty in the 1800s, four had taught at the College, ten were its alumni, eleven served as trustees of the College, and ten were recipients of its honorary degrees. Of the 205 directors and 111 trustees of the Seminary in this period, nearly sixty percent were alumni, members of the faculty, trustees or honorary degree recipients of the College. Just as the members of the Presbyterian Church in many communities generally represented a socially responsible, successful segment of society, so did the membership of the two governing boards of the Seminary. It was also well knit not only by commitments to Presbyterian distinctiveness but in many cases by family ties and close business and financial relationships.

William Henry Green, who himself bequeathed $10,000 to the Seminary for fellowships, was a member of an extensive family (a family distinct from the Ashbel Green family) that provided many directors and trustees as well as extensive financial support to the Seminary. Three uncles were members of the Board of Trustees: Henry Woodhull Green, from 1833 to 1877, and vice president and then president of the board from 1855 to 1877; John Cleve Green, from 1853 to 1875 and financial agent from 1856 to 1867; and Caleb Smith Green, Jr., from 1876 to 1891. In addition, three cousins were board members: Charles Ewing Green, from 1877 to 1897; Elmer Ewing Green, from 1891 to 1909; and Henry Woodhull Green II, from 1905 to 1930. But the intra-family involvement with the Seminary does not end with the Greens. They were inter-married with the Duffields, the Ewings, the Hamills, the Kennedys, the Libbeys, the Van Cleves, the Woodhulls and others who had members serving on the boards.

Of the immediate Green relations John Cleve Green was in a financial position to be the most generous, and this he was with the several millions of dollars that he contributed in his life time or through his estate to the Seminary, the College, and to the nearby Lawrenceville School. Not only did he have a family relationship with many of the board members, he also enjoyed a close business and financial relationship in New York City with such men as James Lenox, Alexander Stuart and his brother, Robert L. Stuart, a trustee from 1847 to 1882. Furthermore, his pastor in New York was George Potts, '22, a seminary director from 1836 to 1864. The Green, the Lenox, and the Stuart families were the largest donors to Princeton Seminary in the nineteenth century.

John Cleve Green had first been successful in the China trade and then, after marrying into a family of wealth, had made prudent investments in banking and railroads, enterprises that were expanding in the middle of the century. A man of deep religious faith, he and his wife, after the death of each of their three young children, distributed most of their wealth to charitable causes.

The brothers Alexander and Robert L. Stuart inherited a small candy business from their Scottish father. After his death they developed a method of refining sugar by steam on which basis they greatly expanded their business and the source of their wealth. As trustees of the Seminary John Cleve Green, James Lenox, and Robert L. Stuart were privy to its repeated financial requirements, and as generous patrons they repeatedly shared their wealth among the several eleemosynary institutions with which they were associated, one of which was Princeton Theological Seminary. After their husbands' deaths Mrs. Green and Mrs. Stuart continued to meet many of the financial needs of the Seminary.

Facilities and Finances

During the second half of the nineteenth century the enrollment of the seminary varied from a low of 102 in 1855 to a high of 263 in 1894 with an average of 131 during the third quarter of the century and an average of 179 in the final quarter. The enrollment, which was almost entirely Scots-Irish Presbyterian, did not maintain a steady progression but fluctuated. During the Civil War it was higher immediately following the reunion of 1869 until the Seminary encountered increasing competition from other seminaries, several of which provided more desirable accommodations. Concurrent with construction of new buildings on the campus the enrollment again increased and then remained near its peak into the 1890s. Throughout this period graduates of Princeton College comprised approximately twenty-five percent of the enrollment while those from minority groups represented a very small percentage of the student body.

Black students were welcome to enroll in the Seminary but few did so during the nineteenth century, even after emancipation following the Civil War. Among the few who did were several contemporaries who later in their lives made remarkable social contributions. Matthew Anderson '77 dedicated his life to urban improvements in the city of Philadelphia. Francis J. Grimké '78, as a pastor and outspoken advocate of rights for minorities, provided similar leadership to his people in Washington, D.C., while his classmate, Hugh M. Browne, served as a teacher and director of what became Cheyney State University. Daniel W. Culp '79 conducted pastoral duties before entering medical school and then caring for patients in several different communities. Thomas M. Stewart '81 followed a different path by teaching in Liberia before studying and then practicing law in New York and Hawaii. The name of William A. Byrd '94, who was with Grimké one of the founders of the National Association for the Advancement of Colored People, is still remembered at the seminary a century later. In 1987 his son established in his memory a prize to be awarded "to the graduating senior who has contributed in an outstanding way to the Seminary community during his or her student days."

It was not the appearance of minority students, whose presence was a constructive influence on the campus, but fluctuations in the total enrollment that created strains. These strains affected both academic and financial planning. The latter involved additional expenses in those years when dormitory accommodations on the campus were insufficient to house all students and when the Seminary was required, as a result of its policy of charging no room rent, to subsidize the room rentals for students who were housed in private homes in town. A second dormitory became an obvious necessity.

In recognition of this need Mrs. Isabella McLanahan Brown of Baltimore indicated to her pastor, John C. Backus '35, her intention to provide the necessary funds for another dormitory, but the initiation of military hostilities in 1860 dissuaded her from fulfilling her promise. Although a Pennsylvanian by birth she was loyal to her adopted city where she and her recently deceased, wealthy husband, George Brown, had made numerous civic contributions. Her disinclination was reversed when Professor McGill was stimulated to write to her by the presence on the campus of a southern lad in the grey uniform of a Confederate soldier attending classes and mingling on a friendly basis with northern students. That student was Henry Branch '65 from Richmond, Virginia; and the news of his reception at a northern institution during hostilities convinced this generous lady to contribute $30,000 toward the construction of Brown Hall. The building, which was designed by J. B. Huber of Newark and completed in 1865, actually cost $41,176. It housed 80 students and was within a few years equipped with gas heat for which the students each paid $10 a session. A decade later Mrs. Brown contributed another $3,000 toward improvements in the building which in 1880 involved the installation of sanitary conveniences.

With the growth in the enrollment other facilities were needed. In their enterprising manner the students themselves met part of these needs by constructing in 1859 a wooden gymnasium, named Langdonic Hall, which they continued to use until 1893 when Hodge Hall was built on its site. The students could not, however, provide for additional lecture and classroom space. This need Alexander and Robert L. Stuart met when they acquired the necessary land, engaged William A. Potter, later United States Supervising Architect, to design the building, and in 1876 at a cost of over $100,000 donated Stuart Hall. This building has for well over a century tangibly demonstrated the interest that the Stuarts maintained in the seminary. It does not adequately identify their exceptional generosity of upwards of a million dollars that funded the Stuart Professorship, purchased faculty houses, assisted in operational expenses, increased the general endowment and culminated in

Mrs. Robert L. Stuart's bequest of $300,000, part of which was assigned to the costs of constructing Hodge Hall in 1893.

Meanwhile, both Alexander Hall and Miller Chapel, which were so renamed in 1893, required major rehabilitation. To meet the costs John Cleve Green offered to provide the necessary funds. Work on the chapel had been completed and the seminary had been reimbursed approximately $6,700, but the work on Alexander Hall was only begun when Green died in 1875. The resulting financial worries that his death caused the Seminary trustees were soon allayed. To Green's executors an offer was a commitment to be fulfilled. The total cost of $21,745 to repair Alexander Hall was paid from the estate which later contributed $150,000 in addition to the $50,000 that Green had specified in his will. These gifts were only an extension of his previous munificences. In his lifetime he and his wife had donated a faculty house and land, had established the Helena Professorship, and had made frequent contributions to the financial operations of the Seminary.

The third major donor to the seminary in the nineteenth century, James Lenox, expressed both his bibliophilism and his interest in the Seminary by appointing Richard Morris Hunt to design a red brick library and two faculty houses that he had constructed on land he had purchased, the total cost of which was $100,000. All of this he donated to the seminary in 1879, thirty-six years after he had contributed the first library, a Gothic-revival styled building that continued to provide reference services while the newer building housed the circulating library. This family's generosity was further enhanced when his sister, Miss Henrietta Lenox, donated an additional $100,000 after her brother's death in 1880, and on her death a decade later left a bequest for an equal amount.

With the addition of these new buildings the campus with its adjacent faculty houses had undergone considerable change and had become an attraction for molesters and pilferers. As a deterrence to intruders a night watchman was employed in 1878. To provide a more dependable water supply than was available from its own wells, in the early 1880s the seminary helped finance the installation of underground water pipes connected to the recently organized Princeton Water Company. Further improvements were instituted in the 1890s.

In that latter decade Mercer Street, which bisected the campus, was for the first time graded and macadamized, that is, paved. Electric lights were installed by the borough at the entrances to the campus. The Seminary buildings were connected to the municipal sewer system, and bathtubs, water closets and urinals were installed in Alexander Hall, the latter on a trial basis. Outdoor privies, including "Old Egypt" behind Miller Chapel, were removed. Late in the decade electricity replaced gas for lighting in Alexander Hall, and the first telephone on the campus was installed in the library.

These amenities, which were soon considered necessities, did not resolve the need for even more dormitory space to house students, some of whom were still forced to reside in rooming houses. Following a recommendation of the faculty in 1889 the Board of Trustees authorized the construction of an additional dormitory that was completed in 1893 based on the architectural plans drawn by R. H. Robertson, a student and later partner of Potter. The costs of construction amounting to $106,200 were provided from the bequest of Mrs. Robert L. Stuart. Consistent with the decision made the previous year to memorialize Archibald Alexander and Samuel Miller by renaming buildings for them, this newest dormitory was named for Charles Hodge.

During this period of the nineteenth century when so much building construction was undertaken at the Seminary there was a continual need for funds to meet faculty salaries and other operating expenses. The minutes of both the Board of Directors and the Board of Trustees attest to their concerns and their endeavors to obtain additional financing. Inflationary forces, larger enrollments, and increased expectations collectively exerted pressures on the two boards, especially the trustees, to raise funds.

In 1851 it was estimated that $20,000 was required to increase the endowment to an adequate total, and this amount was soon realized, primarily from the three principal donors. By the end of the Civil War in 1865 the endowment had more than tripled to over $300,000, and the campus with its several

Student's Dormitory Room, 1908

Jesse M. Corum, Jr. (seated in middle) entertaining fellow students
in his Alexander Hall room

buildings on 14 acres was valued at $118,000. Despite this in-
crease in assets it was decided that $150,000 more should be
raised, and Professor Alexander T. McGill was appointed the
agent to undertake this solicitation. By 1871, when the needs
were reassessed to be $320,000, lack of agreement developed
between the two boards—minor harbingers of the 1920s—and
appeals were temporarily suspended.

With the resumption of solicitations the assets of the Seminary continued to grow so that by the end of the century they
totaled over $2 million with a yearly income from endowment
of some $80,000. Funds had been established to benefit the li-
brary, to finance some one hundred scholarships and a half
dozen professorships, and to endow the first lectureship in
1871, initially financed by and named for Levi P. Stone, a director from 1869 to 1884 and trustee from 1875 to 1884. In addi-

tion, the General Assembly held title to $102,000, the income from which was designated for the benefit of the Seminary. These assets were not sufficient, however, to prevent operating deficits from occurring in many years.

Student Amenities

Throughout its history Princeton Theological Seminary has relied on individual churches and church organizations for support, often centering its appeals on assistance in various forms for the seminary students. Churches responded in various ways, some forming penny clubs as a means of raising funds for the Seminary. In the 1850s, when there were allegations that some graduating seniors were extracting exorbitant prices from entering students for hand-me-down furniture, the faculty proposed that the rooms be furnished by the Seminary. Some churches responded to these appeals with twenty-six rooms being so furnished in the first year. In the latter part of the nineteenth century an interesting response was forthcoming from the ladies of the Fifth Avenue Presbyterian Church in New York. Until 1894 they had furnished the members of each graduating class with a "suit of broadcloth, called a preacher's suit." In that year they decided to change their focus and instead contributed to a loan fund as a means of benefiting students whose personal expenses had also been rising and who would need funds to graduate. Total seminary costs for each student excluding text books were approaching $150 to $200 a year.

A malarial and typhoid epidemic in 1880 which had resulted in several deaths in Princeton, including seminary and college students, had also increased attention to student welfare. Soon thereafter Cornelius R. Agnew, a physician from New York, was engaged to deliver lectures on basic hygiene and health to the seminarians. When the first Isabella McCosh Infirmary was constructed by the College in 1892, William L. Moore '57 donated $2,500 to the building fund as a memorial to his son and namesake and as an endowment to support a bed for ill seminary students.

Although infectious diseases were always a concern, the health of students has more likely been affected in recent years by their nutrition and eating habits. Until 1899 the Seminary endeavored to meet the gastronomical needs of its students in its refectory, or "refractory" as it was often called, but all could not be satisfied. Even with subvention from the Seminary to provide lower costs for meals some students sought other dining locations. Since cooking in dormitory rooms was forbidden, the only recourse was in private boarding houses which in time became the popular student eating clubs. By 1899 the refectory with its aging equipment was closed, possibly partially because of poor management, and eating clubs became a characteristic feature enjoyed by several generations of students.

The history of the Benham Club records that it was organized in October 1879 and named for Mrs. Benham whose "beautiful provisions for our gastronomic demands were noised about and our table would scarce accommodate the number who sought entrance." The stated purposes of this group were to serve "as an eating and social club for the students and alumni of Princeton Theological Seminary, to promote good fellowship and foster friendships among the said students and alumni, and for the general welfare and comfort of the said students and alumni."

The spirit of these clubs, as expressed by one of its seven founders, was recorded in the history of the Friars Club.

In the year 1893 the gastronomical division of the department of my interior revolted at the thought of continuing the punishment of well meaning men by the assaults made upon their stomachs by food of poor quality and poor selection and of insufficient vitamin content.

I had the distinction of proposing to a certain group of congenial spirits, whom I suspected to be of like mind as my own, that we buy our own food and employ a woman to cook it for us, charging each man a fixed sum per week, and designate one the purchasing agent.

Among the groups to be similarly organized were the Adelphian Club in the early 1890s, and in the twentieth century various clubs including Benedict, Boors, Calvin, Canterbury,

Benham Club
Members assembled at the clubhouse
in the early 1900s

Epicurean, Irish, Seminary, and Warfield. Leasing or owning houses adjacent to the campus and engaging a cateress these clubs provided an opportunity to establish congenial friendships, a haven for conviviality, and a means of inculcating social habits in potential ministers of the church. Not always successful in these student-run operations some clubs closed, some merged, but some continued to operate until the opening of the Campus Center in 1952 at which time they all ceased operations and transferred what assets they then had to the Seminary. The Center was later renamed the Mackay Campus Center.

Curricular Developments

The deaths of Charles Hodge in 1878 and of his son Archibald Alexander Hodge in 1886 in no way diminished the commitment of Princeton Theological Seminary to the Reformed faith as espoused by the Old School adherents. If for no other reason the continued presence of William Henry Green and the appointment to the faculty of Benjamin Breckenridge Warfield in 1887 assured theological constancy. However, changes and additions were introduced in the curriculum, albeit slowly, during the latter part of the nineteenth century.

In the 1870s the academic program included course work in Hebrew, the Old and New Testament, church history and history of religion, the theory and practice of homiletics, elocution, pastoral and ecclesiastical theology, apologetics and ethics, and systematic theology. A few students were permitted to enroll at the College in various elective courses including revealed religion and ethnological science, revealed religion and metaphysical science, and philosophy. This last course was taught by President McCosh, and later by John Grier Hibben '86, subsequently president of the University from 1912 to 1932. The small seminary faculty also offered a few special extra-curricular courses, such as Arabic, Chaldee, and Sanskrit.

Two decades later when the size of the faculty had been enlarged the curriculum was expanded slightly by the addition of Greek and New Testament Biblical theology, and an increase in the hours of instruction devoted to apologetics, church history, and systematic theology. The variety of college courses that could be elected was also expanded to include logic, philosophy, psychology, and science among others. The history of law was taught by Woodrow Wilson when he was a college professor, and before he was president of the University and later president of the United States.

Following approval by the New Jersey legislature in 1897 for seminaries to grant degrees, Princeton Seminary instituted the policy of awarding the bachelor of divinity degree, many years later identified as the master of theology degree, to college graduates who had also completed a three year seminary program and subsequently "a one year's course of extra-curriculum study at this Seminary." Shortly thereafter cooperation with Princeton University, as it was renamed in 1896, was expanded even further to permit a few seminary students to enroll concurrently in the College as graduate students and after four terms receive a master of arts degree.

Even with these changes there were a few students who resisted some of the Seminary requirements that they considered to be too restrictive. Walter Lowrie, for whom the University president's house is now named, was an exceptionally brilliant seminarian but annoyingly difficult for the faculty. The winner of a prize to study in Germany and able to conduct classes in New Testament Greek for other students, which he did on occasion, he was nevertheless so irregular in his class attendance that he was formally reprimanded by both the faculty and the Board of Directors.

Among others who became unsympathetic to the Princeton theology were the two later famous brothers, Henry and Paul van Dyke, both professors at Princeton University. Paul '84 departed from the faculty of the Seminary in 1892 unsympathetic with what he pereceived to be its theological restrictions. For his part, Henry '77, convinced of the validity of evolution, endeavored to encourage the Seminary to accept science in the spirit of cooperation and not as a threat. It was Henry who, because of his short height, had been encouraged by Charles Hodge to drink beer as a stimulus for growth. It was he to whom the seniors at the University would sing "Here's to Henry, the brother of Paul; he has a large head, but he's not very tall." Although these two men differed with the theological approach of the Seminary neither was chastised for irregular class attendance.

Student attendance at classes, which were conducted largely as lectures, and their presence at examinations had, however, been troublesome issues for the faculty for many years. In 1865 and again in 1885 the number of non-excused absences had become so excessive that actions by the directors were required. Whether or not these actions were effective was not recorded in the minutes of the board meetings.

Part of the reason for the irregular class attendance may have been attributed to the attitude of the faculty as recorded in the minutes of the Board of Directors as of April 27, 1869.

The system of grading adopted in colleges and schools has never been introduced into our Theological Seminaries, and is at variance with the principle upon which they have been conducted from the beginning. This is to rely upon the students' own sense of obligation rather than upon external and artificial stimulus for diligence and devotion to study. We would greatly deprecate the substitution of ambitious rivalry and love of preferment for a sense of duty, as the motives by which the students are to be mainly educated. Those who are not sufficiently under the control of higher motives to be faithful to their obligations in the Seminary, and whose attention to study can only be secured by the stimulus of grades give little promise of ministerial zeal or efficiency hereafter.

At this time the students' academic progress was based only on their attendance record and the score on their examinations; and the latter were conducted orally by a committee of the directors. As the enrollment increased and as the attendance of the committee members became irregular, written examinations were introduced, and by the 1890s had totally replaced the oral presentations. By 1894 the number of written examinations had overwhelmed the directors and they requested a review of only those that the faculty considered unsatisfactory.

Lest later generations should doubt the spirituality of the Princeton seminarians of the latter nineteenth century it may be noted that the catalogues repeatedly announced each year the schedule of religious exercises to be as follows.

Daily prayers, which every student is expected to attend, are conducted in the morning by members of the Senior Class, and in the evenings by the Professors.

On Sabbath mornings the Professors preach in rotation in the Seminary Chapel. In the afternoon a Conference is held in the Oratory, at which the Professors conduct the discourse on a subject previously announced, and the students conduct the devotional exercises.

Missionary meetings are held every Sabbath evening among the students. The concert of prayer on the first Monday of each month is under the direction of the Professors.

In addition, students frequently conducted religious meetings in the Princeton area, taught Sunday Schools, and continued their interest in missionary work by forming the Princeton Missionary Society in the 1880s, and then in 1893 establishing the Students' Lectureship on Missions. They invited speakers to the campus, not always to the liking of the faculty. In 1870 the senior students had the temerity to ask without prior faculty approval the popular preacher Henry Ward Beecher to address them a week before their graduation. Employing diplomatic and judicious restraint Charles Hodge invited Beecher, whose relatively liberal and evangelical theology did not coincide with the Princeton traditions, to meet with students in his own home. This incident occurred, however, five years before the famous trial of Beecher for adultery and two years before the semi-centennial celebration of Hodge's long tenure on the faculty.

The Princeton Theology

No single individual was identified more intimately with the Calvinistic theology of the nineteenth century than Charles Hodge. Nor was anyone in the Presbyterian Church in that era held with such affection, respect, even awe. Why could one professor be so influential? Leonard J. Trinterud '38 has provided an observation.

But whence the Hodge of the myth? Given a man of strong personality in a prominent seminary, for many years the leading mind of that school, idolized by students and alumni, in control of a privately owned journal of great influence, a writer of both popular and professional books, with a wide correspondence in various parts of the country, a man human enough to enter deeply into the lives of his friends—in short, given a man so gifted and so situated, it was inevitable that he should build and guide a large and influential group of disciples. (Kerr, *Sons of the Prophets*, p. 205)

In recognition of Hodge's theological leadership a special convocation was convened in 1872 at which a number of his numerous admirers spoke eloquently of his extensive contributions to the Seminary and the Church during a period of fifty years. On this occasion his many friends and alumni of the Seminary, nearly three thousand of whom would have been his students, contributed $45,000 to establish a professorship in his honor and an additional $15,000 as a personal gift to him. In concluding this widely heralded convocation he spoke with respect of his two predecessors and of his unequivocal commitment to God's self-revelation in the Bible.

Again, Drs. Alexander and Miller were not speculative men. They were not given to new methods or new theories. They were content with the faith once delivered to the saints. I am not afraid to say that a new idea never originated in the Seminary. Their theological method was very simple. The Bible is the word of God. That is to be assumed or proved. If granted; then it follows, that what the Bible says, God says. That ends the matter. (Hodge, *Semi-Centennial*, p. 52)

Toward the end of his life Hodge edited his carefully written and consistently reasoned lectures that were published under the title of *Systematic Theology*. These influential volumes represented what was called the Princetopon Theology and provided an historical record of the premise on which he and many others based their religious beliefs. Addressing the issue of the infallibility and divine authority of Scriptures, Hodge wrote:

. . . the common doctrine of the Church is, and ever has been, that inspiration was an influence of the Holy Spirit on the minds of certain select men, which rendered them the organs of God for the infallible communication of his mind and will. They were in a sense the organs of God, that what they said God said. (Hodge, *Systematic Theology*, vol. I, p. 154)

The view presented above is known as the doctrine of plenary inspiration. Plenary is opposed to partial. The Church doctrine denies that inspiration is confined to parts of the Bible; and affirms that it applies to all the books of the sacred canon. It denies that the sacred writers were merely partially inspired; it asserts that they were fully inspired as to all that they teach, whether of doctrine or fact. This of course does not imply that the sacred writers were infallible except for the special purposes for which they were employed. They were not imbued with plenary knowledge. As to all matters of science, philosophy, and history, they stood on the same level with their contemporaries. They were infallible only as teachers, and when acting as the spokesmen of God. (ibid, p. 165)

Hodge's theological convictions, which represented the basis of what many others called the Princeton Theology, provided a solid foundation for those who devoutly accepted the authority of the Bible, but this theology allowed for no flexibility in its guiding premises. As Forrest G. Wood noted "the controversy between the religious conviction that the Bible is the revealed word of God and the academic proposition that it is the 'human literary product of an ancient socio-political and religious community' cannot be resolved because there is no common ground of reconciliation." (Wood, p. 109)

Reflecting on Hodge's theological position, one might more than a century later and in a different social era incorrectly assume that this erudite professor was an austere, forbidding individual. In fact, he was known to be "sunny, genial, kindly and tolerant." As described by William Berryman Scott, who was raised in Hodge's home and who later was a professor at Princeton University, there was "the most unrestrained jollity and fun, with repartee, and good-natured banter . . . but there was never any quarrelling, gossip, or ill-natured talk, or detraction of any one." (Scott, W.B., p. 8)

Hodge was a moderator of the General Assembly of the Presbyterian Church, a member and president of both its Board of Education and its Board of Foreign Missions, and a trustee of the College of New Jersey for twenty-seven years. These responsibilities were all religiously oriented and did not expose him to the social changes resulting from immigration, industrialization, urbanization, western expansion accompanied by increasing diversity. Those individuals who were beginning to emphasize the social gospel considered Princeton Seminary to be more interested in book learning, in cultivating gentlemen, and in serving the upper classes. For his part Hodge was concerned with combating infidelity and protecting Biblical truth, continually espousing an interpretation of the Bible that became known as the Princeton Theology. This singleness of conviction, which was translated into an homogeneous Presbyterian doctrine, was apparent in the Seminary's support of the heresy trials of Charles A. Briggs, Arthur Cushman McGiffert, and Henry Preserved Smith, professors at Lane and Union seminaries—trials that could have foretold the wider divisions in the church to explode in the 1920s.

Hodge's unequaled position of widespread admiration and respect was again demonstrated when the General Assembly convened in Baltimore in 1877. Visiting in Washington at the time but too weak to attend the meeting at which he was to be recognized at a special ceremony, Hodge was doubly honored by the Assembly whose members traveled to Washington in a body especially to greet him.

A century later Hodge was largely forgotten except by historians among whom were two Princeton Seminary professors. They wrote from the perspective of a later period and long after the restructuring of the Seminary in the early 1930s. Their comments not only present their perspective of Charles Hodge but they imply their own theological emphases that prevailed while they were active members of the faculty of the Seminary.

In 1983 Lefferts A. Loetscher '28 wrote that Hodge

failed to view history as a continually transforming process . . . This static concept of history, which resisted the newer concept of process, became one of the central characteristics of the Old Princeton Theology and, along with Biblical inerrancy and unwillingness to compromise denominational distinctives, contributed to an increasing ideal of resistance to change. (Loetscher, *Facing the Enlightenment*, p. 160)

Twenty years before this observation by Loetscher, Hugh T. Kerr, Jr. had presented the views of many members of the faculty of that decade, views that have subsequently continued to prevail.

The temptation at Princeton was more in the direction of cloistered scholasticism patterned after post-Reformation orthodoxy. This was a highly cerebral theological tradition, but it often resulted in an intellectualism unrelated to vital religion, the currents of secular and scientific thought, and the practical life of the Church. It is no secret that many contemporary professors at the Seminary feel completely out of touch theologically with their predecessors of a generation or more ago on such issues as Biblical criticism, apologetics, the sacraments, and the interpretation of the Westminster Confession of Faith. (Kerr, *Sons of the Prophets*, p. xii)

Further revisions in the Westminster Confession of Faith did not have to wait, however, until the twentieth century. In 1892 the General Assembly acquiesced to the wishes of a majority of its members and approved some liberation in its strict provisions but not in its stance on Biblical authority. At the same time signs of independence were expressed by both boards of the Seminary which, after many separate and joint sessions, rejected proposals by the Assembly which would have strengthened its power over the boards' decisions.

But changes in church doctrine were slow to evolve and, as anticipated by John F. Hageman, would be resisted by the Seminary for many more years in the future. Hageman, a local lawyer, historian, son-in-law of Samuel Miller, and a trustee from 1851–1892, was in a position to observe at close hand the historically conservative stance of the Seminary.

The class of independent and advanced thinkers who believe in human progress, in the better understanding of the Bible, and in the better use of language, is small in the Presbyterian Church, and will not, for many years at least, cause a reaction against the conservative school at Princeton. The Seminary is well anchored therefore in the Calvinistic doctrines—otherwise known as the Princeton Theology. (Hageman, p. 376)

The teachings of Archibald Alexander and Samuel Miller, which were expanded, systematically organized, and espoused by Charles Hodge, were staunchly maintained by William Henry Green in the nineteenth century, and by Hodge's disciple, Benjamin Breckenridge Warfield, into the twentieth century. The legacy was then assumed by the fiery John Gresham Machen '05 and his adherents who, only after a determined and bitter struggle, finally had to succumb to the intensifying winds of theological change and depart the Princeton Seminary. In this slow transformation and eventual denouement hundreds of alumni suffered the pain of seeing their alma mater being split in twain.

Alumni in the Missionary Field

The purpose of all professional schools is to prepare their students to practice the professions to which they are committed. In this process each profession, such as law and medicine, endeavors to control the education of its future members so that they will conform to the standards and beliefs of those who have already been graduated. With these principles Princeton Theological Seminary was in its early years sympathetic. The ordained clergy constituted the majority control of the Seminary during its first one hundred years. Its students were inculcated in Presbyterian doctrines and upon graduation dispersed into church work throughout the country and to missions throughout the world. Its graduates constituted the largest body of alumni of any seminary in the United States well into the twentieth century. It was then and still is an impressive institution.

Princeton Seminary has produced over fifty moderators of the General Assemblies of the several Presbyterian denominations, bishops of the Protestant Episcopal Church, founders of colleges and seminaries, professors and teachers for innumerable institutions, pastors by the thousands for churches throughout the land, editors and writers, and foreign missionaries in the hundreds. These men, and now also women, have a bond through the Alumni Association of Princeton Theological Seminary which was re-established on April 24, 1872 at the time of the special convocation for Charles Hodge. It was then declared that all who have been students in the Seminary shall be members, and all professors and board members shall be ex-officio members. The objective of this Association was stated "to be the promotion of brotherly love among its members, and the advancement of the interests of the Seminary." Through its activities alumni and alumnae have been able to maintain a bond that has been especially dear to those who were for years separated from home as they served as missionaries in other continents.

Until 1875 one of every eighteen graduates of the Seminary entered the mission field. By the end of the century the proportion had increased with the majority continuing to have China or India as their destinations. Their lot in life could be precarious. Although not a common happening violent deaths continued to occur. John Edgar Freeman '38 and his wife, and Isidore Loewenthal '54 were each shot to death in India in the middle of the past century. Few others encountered such a deadly reception. Robert Hamill Nassau '59 devoted his life as a medical missionary to the welfare of the natives of different countries in west central Africa. John Wherry '61 died in Peking after spending all his post-seminary years as a missionary in China where Henry Winters Luce '96 served from 1897 to 1927, the latter years as vice president of Peking University.

Whether in Asia, Africa, or the Near East these men with the support of their wives preached Christianity, translated scriptures, taught children, trained natives to be ministers and cared for the sick. William Ambrose Shedd '92, the son of a missionary in Persia, now Iran, returned to succeed his father. Among those who were attracted to the Indians of the North American continent was the legendary Sheldon Jackson '58 whose missionary activities extended the length of all the Rocky Mountain states as well as Alaska and included service with the Board of National Missions.

The Student Volunteer Movement, which was organized in Northfield, Massachusetts in 1886, and the Foreign Missions Conference, which was established in 1893 to reduce competition among the denominations, were compatible with the ethos of Princeton Seminary as enunciated at the Alumni Association meeting in 1876. On that occasion Daniel S. Gregory '60, then professor at the College of Wooster and later president of Lake Forest College, declared that "Princeton Seminary is everywhere known as representing the strict loyalty to the sacred Scriptures as the Word of God, the only and plenarily inspired rule of faith and practice. . . . It has therefore always recognized what the history of the world has demonstrated, that Christianity is the only foundation of a true morality, the only source of permanent information, individual, social and civil, the only builder of a true and worthy manhood."

Of all the seminary alumni none expressed a more persistent

77

PRINCETON SEMINARY MARTYRS

Elijah Parish Lovejoy, 1834
First Martyr for the Freedom of the Press
Died Protecting his Printing Press
from Mob Attack
Alton, Illinois, 1837

John Edgard Freeman, 1838
Robert McMullin, 1854
Shot with their Wives by order of Nana Sahib
Cawnpore, India, 1857

Walter Macon Lowrie, 1840
Drowned by Pirates in the China Sea, 1847

Levi Janvier, 1840
Killed by a Sikh Fanatic
Lodiana, India, 1864

Isidor Loewenthal, 1854
Killed at Peshawur, India, 1864

William Edgar McChesney, 1869
Killed by River Pirates
Canton, China, 1872

William A. Shedd, 1892
Died of Exhaustion Leading Armenian
Christian Refugees
Sian Kala, Persia, 1918

John Rogers Peale '05
Killed with his Wife
Lien Chou, China, 1905

James Joseph Reeb '53
Fatally Beaten
Selma, Alabama, 1965

commitment to the mission field than Robert Elliott Speer '93. Serving as secretary of the Presbyterian Board of Foreign Missions from 1891 to 1937 he traveled far and wide and was recognized as a man with devotion to the Christian faith, dedication to missions, and loyalty to Princeton Theological Seminary. Fortunately for the Seminary he was a member of its governing boards from 1914 to his death in 1947, a period of strain when calm and judicious influence was most needed—personal characteristics which he and others exerted to reorient the Seminary in the direction which it has subsequently pursued.

5

Now It Came To Pass

SAMUEL II

Compared to the issues with which the Presbyterian Church contended in the first decades of the twentieth century the events of the nineteenth century now appear in retrospect to be less momentous than the participants in that earlier period understandably considered them to be. The schism in 1837, the reunion in 1869, the subsequent heresy trials were all traumatic events. They involved deeply felt theological differences, contention for authority, and personality conflicts. With the passage of time they were resolved but not without adding to the heritage of differences between the New Side and the Old Side of the eighteenth century, and the New School and the Old School of the nineteenth century.

The basic divergence of these historical conflicts emerged again in the early twentieth century, this time in the form of an eruption that involved accusations and denunciations couched in the usual terms of religious authority. In the wake of World War I the Presbyterian Church in the United States of America was in turmoil and the epicenter of the strife was Princeton Theological Seminary. During the conflicts of the previous century the Seminary with its conservative inclinations had served as an ameliorating influence. Not so in the conflagration of the 1920s that was inflamed by a bitterly divergent faculty, and by a Board of Directors and a Board of Trustees, each of which supported conflicting points of view.

Because the strife involved a major religious denomination and a leading theological seminary, the national press and the emerging radio provided the public with extensive coverage both of the statements issued by the participants in the fray and of the actions by the General Assembly and other ecclesiastical bodies. At the height of the controversy the issues became trammeled and entwined with personality conflicts. It was a period of considerable controversy and friction from which, one may now observe, Princeton Theological Seminary emerged to be a stronger, more effective and influential institution committed to the education of men and women for different types of positions of religious responsibility in a multi-denominational, multi-racial, and more secular society.

Seminary Governance

Every profession endeavors to control the education of its future members and their admission to professional practice. In the case of those religious denominations that are dependent upon the leadership of their clergy, their governing bodies exercise varying degrees of control over the seminaries that prepare their ministers prior to ordination. When Princeton Theological Seminary was founded in 1812, it was then decided not to compromise the responsibility of ordination exercised by the presbyteries. At the same time, authority to establish and govern the Seminary was jealously established and maintained by the General Assembly.

From time to time the relationship between the General Assembly and its Presbyterian seminaries underwent reviews. In 1870, at the time of the reunion of the New School and the Old School to form the Presbyterian Church in the United States of America, the control by the General Assembly was somewhat modified to permit more authority to the two governing boards of Princeton Seminary, as well as to the boards of several of the other seminaries. Two decades later attention was again directed to the seminaries when in 1892 the General Assembly adopted a resolution that urged its thirteen seminaries to review their status in order to assure that all funds held by the seminaries were restricted to the support of theological education, that their teachings were in accord with approved Presbyterian doctrines, and that the General Assembly retained the power of control over appointments, of disposition of the funds and property of the seminaries, and of their teaching.

For the next several years the members of the two boards of

Princeton Seminary held innumerable formal and informal meetings, separately and jointly, to decide how to respond to the overture of the General Assembly in a positive manner without complying with the implied mandate. The result was merely a proposal which was enacted in 1897 by the New Jersey State legislature that "assured the General Assembly the right to be represented in the courts and to enforce its proper control over the Seminary. . . ." In that same year the legislature enacted separate legislation that authorized seminaries in New Jersey to award bachelor of divinity or bachelor of theology degrees.

Having labored jointly on issues of seminary governance during much of the last decade of the nineteenth century, the two boards realized that the time had arrived when their by-laws should be recodified, especially since the original ones could not be found. Accordingly, a joint committee of three directors and three trustees undertook the assignment and issued a report in 1901, the significant result of which was an amendment to establish the position of president. Adopted by both boards, this action discontinued the practice pursued since 1812 by which the senior member of the faculty had assumed in a very part-time manner the undesignated responsibilities of a chief administrative officer. The action that established the basis for an eventual major change in the governance of the seminary was intended to "promote efficiency in its management," and presumably facilitate greater financial support. It stated that the president "shall be representative of the Seminary before the church; he shall be the administrative agent of the Seminary in matters of order and discipline . . . ," and he shall be elected by the Board of Directors consisting of twenty-one clergy and nine ruling elders. The election was to be subject to veto by the General Assembly. Coincidentally, the creation of the position of president of the Seminary occurred at the same time that a change was being engineered in the presidency of Princeton University.

Following the retirement of James McCosh as president of the College of New Jersey in 1888 the conservative theological members of its Board of Trustees were successful in electing

Francis Landey Patton and Faculty Colleagues, 1908-1909
Front row (left to right): President Patton, William M. Paxton, John
DeWitt; *Middle row*: Geerhardus Vos, William B. Greene, Jr.,
Benjamin B. Warfield; John D. Davis, Robert Dick Wilson;
Back row: Henry W. Smith, Joseph H. Dulles,
William P. Armstrong, J. Oscar Boyd

Professor Francis Landey Patton of the Seminary, a member of
its class of 1865, as his successor. McCosh had in his twenty
year presidency succeeded in reawakening the institution from
its long period of somnolence and in introducing a broader curriculum taught by a faculty that increasingly included professors with advanced degrees in fields other than theology. During Patton's fourteen year tenure this momentum continued.
At least nine new buildings were constructed, including six dormitories and the auditorium Alexander Hall, named for Charles
B. Alexander, the grandson of Archibald Alexander. The Graduate School was organized, the student body was doubled in
size, and the honor system for students was established. During
Patton's presidency one of McCosh's dreams was realized in
1896 when the College of New Jersey was legally renamed
Princeton University.

Despite these obvious accomplishments Patton's presidency

was ended when frustrated members of the faculty, including Woodrow Wilson, his successor as president, and a group of trustees in effect forced his resignation. This occurred in 1902 at a time when the Seminary was seeking its first president to which position Patton was readily elected.

Patton was wedded to an obsolescent college curriculum, one that was pursued in the mid-nineteenth century and which McCosh and his appointees had been endeavoring to revise and expand. Furthermore, most glaring was Patton's lack of interest in administrative responsibilities, many of which he failed to perform or did so inadequately. Despite the inappropriateness of these qualities in the president of a university it is possible that they may have been helpful as he became the first president of a seminary whose curriculum and teaching had changed little from the nineteenth century and whose faculty members, accustomed to their traditional independent mode of operation, would not likely have been receptive to an efficient, forceful administrative officer. This certainly proved to be the case with his successor.

Shortly after Patton's death in 1932 William Hallock Johnson '96, then president of Lincoln University, stated that "Dr. Patton with his keen dialectic and his superb rhetoric was the commanding figure upon the religious platform of his day." Having been elected moderator of the General Assembly in 1878 at the age of thirty-five, Patton was widely sought as a preacher and was a popular lecturer among seminary students whom he taught, first at McCormick Seminary, then after 1881 at Princeton Seminary as the first Stuart Professor of Relations of Philosophy and Science to the Christian Religion. In the latter position he also served as lecturer at the College of New Jersey where he was equally popular with the undergraduates.

Patton was a gracious, urbane gentleman with a sense of humor that was exemplified by his response to an inquiry as to what position he had held at the university—"President, once removed." His sense of humor, however, in no way deflected his commitment to the Calvinistic theology taught by Charles Hodge under whom he had studied. Patton was a strict constructionist and a determined defender of the Presbyterian credal standards. Although he denied that there was a Princeton Theology he proclaimed at the Seminary's centennial celebration in 1912 that "Princeton's boast, if she had ever reason to boast at all, is her unswerving fidelity to the theology of the Reformation. *Semper eadem* is a motto that would well befit her." In 1913 at age seventy with deteriorating eyesight Patton resigned from the presidency, having performed the presidential functions little more than as a senior professor. Returning to his native Bermuda he continued his interest in the Seminary as an inactive member of its boards until his death in 1932.

Divided Responsibilities

During Patton's presidency the structure and governance of the Seminary was reviewed on at least two occasions. In 1906 it was decided that there was no legal reason to alter either the name or the corporate structure. In 1911 at the request of both boards Judge William M. Lanning, a director since 1895 and concurrently a trustee since 1907, was requested to provide an analysis of the specific responsibilities of the General Assembly, the Board of Trustees and the Board of Directors of the Seminary. He reported that (1) the General Assembly had full authority to direct and control the Seminary in all matters that did not contravene the provisions of the State charter granted to the Seminary, (2) the Board of Trustees possessed the authority to receive and hold title to all property, and (3) the powers held by the General Assembly prior to 1870 were at that time vested in the Board of Directors subject to approval or disapproval of the trustees in matters of finance.

Fulfilling its responsibility the Board of Directors designated the venerable and erudite Benjamin B. Warfield as acting president when Patton resigned in 1913. A year later when the board gave formal consideration to the election of a permanent president it was expected that Warfield would be nominated, as he was; but he was not the only nominee. The nomination of J. Ross Stevenson, a director since 1902, presented the board with a choice between two quite disparate individuals whose personalities were bound to clash, as they did during the following half dozen years. It was not an easy choice for a board whose chairman, Ethelbert D. Warfield, was a brother of one of the nominees, and many of whose members shared an inflexible commitment to the Princeton Theology. Two sessions of the board were required on June 11, 1914 to resolve the debate which was concluded with the selection of Stevenson, a choice that many directors woefully regretted a decade later during the theological turbulence that afflicted the Presbyterian Church in the 1920s.

A graduate of Washington and Jefferson College and McCormick Seminary, Stevenson had served as pastor of a congregation in Sedalia, Missouri, before returning to McCormick as a professor from 1894 to 1902. He then became pastor of the Fifth Avenue Presbyterian Church in New York which had many associations with Princeton Seminary commencing with its founding in 1812. Seven of his predecessors had served as members of the Board of Directors, two of whom had also been on the faculty: James Waddell Alexander and Stevenson's immediate predecessor, George T. Purves '76. From New York Stevenson was called in 1909 to the Brown Memorial Church in Baltimore, the edifice that was a gift of Mrs. George (Isabella) Brown, donor of Brown Hall at Princeton Seminary.

Stevenson possessed both academic and pastoral experience as well as historical and contemporary associations with the Seminary. From service in various capacities on different boards of the General Assembly he had wide associations throughout the church which elected him moderator in 1915. Furthermore, as an advocate of ecumenicity he was active in the Federal Council of Churches. Following his retirement in 1936 from the presidency of the Seminary, the concept of the World Council of Churches, which was later organized in 1948, was devised during the time that the Archbishop of Canterbury, the Most Reverend William Temple, was a guest in his home.

Aside from personality conflicts, which inevitably emerged, especially with Warfield and later with J. Gresham Machen, Stevenson's differences with the faculty and then the Board of Directors basically coincided with the factionalism that was occurring throughout the church. He believed that the Seminary should serve all of the church and not merely those who insisted on the infallibility of the Bible and strict Calvinistic doctrine. In contrast, the majority of both the faculty and the directors considered that they had a religious obligation to maintain inviolably what they considered to be true Calvinism and that the other Presbyterian related seminaries, of which there were 19 in 1924, could provide diluted theological training if they chose to do so.

One element in this emerging struggle was the corporate structure of Princeton Seminary. In 1923 the General Assembly proposed that the Seminary be governed by one, not two boards. This issue was debated over a period of several years during which time tensions and acrimony increased, not only in the Seminary but throughout the church similar to the internal church struggles that the Presbyterians encountered in the eighteenth and nineteenth centuries.

The trustees favored the creation of one board and the directors strenuously opposed. The composition of the boards provides one clue. In 1926, for example, less than one-half of the trustees were ministers of the Gospel. Of the clergy members most were Princeton Seminary graduates, several of whom were under forty-five years of age. In contrast, all but a few of the directors were clergy, most of whom were also graduates of the seminary but only one of whom was under fifty years of age. Three of the oldest directors had studied under Charles Hodge, and the others under William Henry Green or Benjamin B. Warfield. In this same year of 1926 the average age of the nine professors on the faculty was sixty-two, three of whom were in their seventies and the youngest of whom was fifty. All but one were graduates of the seminary as were the two assistant professors, Machen and Oswald T. Allis, both in the class of 1905.

The directors and the majority of the faculty were determined to maintain the nineteenth century theological heritage of the Seminary for which they sincerely considered themselves to be the custodians. To them a single board would destroy their ability to maintain their sacred trust. In this light one may appreciate the intensity with which they responded to any actions that would weaken their position. Only after extensive negotiations and several years of public controversy was the issue of the corporate structure of the Seminary resolved. By action of the General Assembly in 1929 a single Board of Trustees was created consisting of one-third members nominated by the old Board of Directors, one-third by the old Board of Trustees, and one-third by a special committee subject to endorsement of the General Assembly. The new self-perpetuating board of thirty-three members, which held its first meeting in January 1930, was granted additional authority including the power, after a full hearing and investigation, to remove the president or professors without recourse to the Assembly. The authority of the president was also enlarged and more adequately defined.

Denominational Strife

The strains and tensions that prevailed at the Seminary during Stevenson's administration were not a series of isolated events but part of the larger evolution that had over many decades been transforming society in which all religious denominations, including the Presbyterian Church, were engulfed. In the 1870s Washington Gladden, now remembered as the author of the hymn *O Master, Let Me Walk with Thee*, proclaimed, what Stephen Colwell had earlier insisted, that the church had a serious responsibility to face the economic inequities of an industrializing society. Soon thereafter Walter Rauschenbusch was preaching a gospel of redemption not only of individuals but also of institutions and social systems. Recognition of the teaching of these and other preachers, which became known as the social gospel, was first officially recognized by the Presbyterian Church as early as 1904 when it established a Department of Church and Labor with a full-time secretary. To these developments Princeton Seminary responded with field trips for students to observe inner-city conditions in Philadelphia and New York and participation in the development of modest social programs in Princeton and Trenton.

The pronouncement, however, of a near neighbor, Robert W.

Rogers, professor at Drew Seminary, exerted no apparent influence in Princeton. Speaking at the 80th anniversary of McCormick Seminary in 1909, Rogers declared—

There is too much sensitiveness and dread of heresy. Somebody is turned out, or fails of re-election, or receives properly accredited hints to resign, or is simply pounded because he is reputed to have said or thought something inconsistent with the interpretation of the Bible or creed which somebody else holds. Under such pressure scholarship cannot flourish. These creeds of ours must be a poor company if they cannot stand a bit of a shake now and again. Every first-class institution is entitled to a little heresy here and there to keep it from stagnation. (Rogers, p. 95)

Responding to a request for advice from Harris Elliott Kirk, who had been offered a professorship of homiletics at the seminary, which incidentally he declined, Stevenson wrote in 1909 when he was a director "that Princeton Seminary has still a great influence in the Northern Church. This influence, however, has been on the wane for several years past, largely because the Professors have gotten out of touch with the church and look upon the Seminary more as a conservator of the past than a servant of the present." (Miller, D.G., p. 405) To a similar inquiry Woodrow Wilson replied that "there can be no doubt that the Seminary does in some large degree deserve the reputation which it has for resisting in an unreasonable degree the liberalizing tendencies of the time. . . . It is, nevertheless, a noble institution which needs nothing so much as new blood and to which it is quite conceivable that new blood may bring a broader life." (ibid, p. 409) Wilson's diagnosis proved to be accurate but over two decades were required before a cure could be provided, and during that period much emotional blood was spilled.

As with all major military conflicts, World War I stimulated in its aftermath another period of great social change. Labor strife and bombings were resumed. Women's suffrage was adopted. Prohibition of alcoholic beverages was attempted. Secularism was expanding. Added to these forces and those that were already prevalent before the war was the Russian revolution and the fanatical fear of Bolshevism that permeated the consciousness and affected the actions of the American people for over seventy years. Within this social milieu the Presbyterians struggled in an agonizing manner to adapt their basic religious beliefs to the turbulent twentieth century. Samuel H. Miller, dean of the Harvard Divinity School, had noted that "In every age, embarrassed by the incongruities between its heritage and the common way of life . . . , religion has a hard time of it." (Miller, S.H.) In the 1920s no denomination experienced a more tumultuous period of modification and revision than the Presbyterians.

In an endeavor to reaffirm their Calvinistic heritage and to deter a movement toward diversity, conservatives, who were a majority in the Presbyterian Church at that time, induced the General Assembly in 1910 and again in 1916 to identify five doctrines that were essential to the faith of the church: (1) the inspiration and inerrancy of Scripture, (2) the virgin birth of Christ, (3) the death of Christ as an offering to satisfy divine justice, (4) the resurrection of the physical body of Christ, and (5) the supernatural character of the miracles performed by Christ. In 1923, when the General Assembly reiterated its support of these principles for the third time, a petition, known as the Auburn Affirmation, collected the signature of approximately 1,300 Presbyterian clergy challenging the right of the General Assembly to dictate such restrictions and to delimit diversity in a church body that had since 1870 combined New School and Old School Presbyterians, and since 1906 Cumberland Presbyterians. The petitioners also objected strenuously to the endeavors of the Philadelphia Presbytery to restrict the pulpit in Presbyterian churches to those whose beliefs conformed to the adopted five doctrines.

This issue was raised when in May 1922 the Baptist minister, Harry Emerson Fosdick, preaching at the First Presbyterian Church in New York, spoke on the subject "Shall the Fundamentalists Win?" Contrasting the differences between fundamentalist and liberal theology he proposed solutions to resolve the expanding conflict. His sermon was printed and given wide circulation by Ivy L. Lee, the public relations advisor for John

D. Rockefeller who financed the construction of the Riverside Church in New York where Fosdick became a nationally known preacher. Fosdick's contentions were reiterated several years later by the widely quoted Presbyterian clergyman, Henry Sloane Coffin, who was president of Union Theological Seminary in New York. Coffin chastised the church for focusing too narrowly on individual aspects of the Bible to the detriment of its social components. He also strongly supported the ordination by the New York Presbytery of several candidates who in all conscience could not endorse the five doctrines prescribed by the General Assembly. By 1925 the Assembly did admit the legitimacy of some diversity of theology.

Although the incidents here cited were centered in the eastern part of the nation they agitated the entire church which by 1925 numbered 1.8 million communicants, ten thousand ordained ministers, and a similar number of churches. One may now consider it to be remarkable that a major schism in the church did not then occur as happened in each of the preceding two centuries. But a schism did develop in Princeton Theological Seminary which became the major center of attention of the General Assembly at each of its sessions during the latter part of that decade.

A Seminary Asunder

The Seminary at Princeton represented in microcosm the Presbyterian church at large; that is, with at least one exception. The church recognized and admitted earlier than the Seminary that both the Bible and the Presbyterian theological standard, namely the Westminster Confession, could also be interpreted to teach interdenominational inclusiveness. In this spirit of inclusiveness serious consideration was given by some Presbyterians at the end of World War I to the development of a constructive plan of union with several other evangelical denominations. The ensuing discussions, which were supported by Stevenson and a minority of the Seminary faculty, inflamed the already agitated J. Gresham Machen who throughout the remainder of the decade led the forces that struggled in vain to maintain the Seminary's policies and its commitment to the Calvinism with which he was familiar and to which he was deeply committed.

The struggles which created exhausting agonies for all within and many without the Seminary during this period included not merely theological differences and control of the education of future ministers, but also conflicts of authority between administration and faculty, and the inevitable corollary of intense friction among different personalities. Extensive accounts of these developments have been so thoroughly reported in numerous histories that it would be redundant to retell them in detail. It is sufficient in this narrative merely to mention some of the individuals who were widely identified as major participants in this human drama; or, one might say, near tragedy.

After graduation from the Seminary in 1905 followed by study in Germany, J. Gresham Machen joined the faculty, appointed first as an instructor and then an assistant professor in New Testament. He was recognized as a brilliant, stimulating teacher who was very popular among the students. Upon the death of Benjamin Warfield in 1921 Machen presumed to act as the guardian of the Princeton Theology proclaiming "that modern liberalism was not only a different religion from Christianity but belonged to a totally different class of religion altogether." (Longfield, p. 29) He considered that the most honest and responsible solution to the theological division in the church would be for the liberals to admit their apostasy, withdraw, and even join the Unitarians. (Hart)

Supporting Machen's theological stance was Clarence E. Macartney who had delivered an ardent rebuttal to Fosdick's attempt at resolution of the fundamentalist-modernist controversies. Macartney was a Princeton Seminary classmate of Machen, a director of the Seminary, an accomplished preacher, who was elected Moderator of the General Assembly in 1924 with the active support of the majority of members of the faculty of the Seminary in a contest with Charles R. Erdman, their fellow faculty member.

Some months later the directors of the seminary offered Macartney the professorship of apologetics and Christian ethics that was being vacated by Professor William B. Greene, Jr. After a period of deliberation Macartney declined the offer, following which the Board of Directors then approved the promotion of Machen to this position and reported its action to the General Assembly in 1926. At this session of the Assembly strong opposition was presented by Stevenson and Erdman, the latter having been elected moderator succeeding Macartney. Consequently, action was deferred by the Assembly with respect to Machen's promotion, and this fact only added to the various festering sores that were afflicting the Seminary and the church during this turbulent decade.

Charles Erdman was a seminary graduate in the class of 1891 following which he held pastorates in the Philadelphia Presbytery and was a director of the Seminary before his election to the faculty in 1906 as Professor of Practical Theology. His appointment gave recognition to the need to broaden the curriculum and include instruction in Christian education, evangelism, homiletics, pastoral care, polity, and especially the English Bible for which the students had been petitioning. Erdman was conservative in his theology, evangelistic in purpose, and tolerant in the spirit of Archibald Alexander. His sincere religious convictions, blended with a friendly, gracious and gentlemanly manner, encouraged wide respect which he enjoyed throughout the Presbyterian Church.

The strains between Machen and Erdman were accentuated by their association with the First Presbyterian Church of Princeton. Machen's appointment as supply minister in 1923 received notoriety when Henry Van Dyke, former director of the Seminary, moderator of the General Assembly in 1902 and subsequently United States Ambassador to the Netherlands, publicly announced that he was wasting no more time "in listening to such dismal, bilious travesty of the Gospel. Until he [Machen] is done, count me out, and give up my pew in the church. We want to worship Christ our Savior." (Link p. 94–95) He did not return until Erdman was appointed the pastor in 1924, a pastorate which Erdman served until 1934 concurrently with his professorship at the Seminary.

The other major incident involved action by the students at

the Seminary who shared the theological orientation of Machen and of the majority of the faculty. These students took steps to withdraw in 1924 from the student association of theological seminaries and form a more conservative evangelical organization with a chapter at Princeton. Intimately related to this development that represented a division in the student body was the selection of Professor Robert Dick Wilson as the faculty advisor, supplanting Erdman, who had held the position for nearly twenty years. This was interpreted as a direct personal assault on Erdman.

These incidents were symptomatic of the atmosphere that permeated Princeton Seminary whose two boards provided a further discordant note. In 1924 Stevenson submitted a report to the directors which concluded with a request that a special committee be created to study and report on the internal affairs of the Seminary. Over the succeeding five years this request was followed by formal action of the Board of Trustees expressing confidence in Stevenson and his administration, by the creation of the first of several successive committees of the General Assembly to investigate and report on the Seminary, by the submission of petitions signed by thousands of individuals, by resolutions adopted by the Alumni Association, by formal opposition on the part of the directors and the majority of the faculty to the recommendations of the General Assembly's special committee, by widely distributed pamphlets written by Machen, Stevenson and others arguing their respective positions, and by demands on the part of some directors, led by Ethelbert Warfield, for Stevenson's resignation.

In the midst of all this turmoil Robert E. Speer was elected moderator by unanimous vote at the 1927 General Assembly. He shared with many others in the Assembly a conservative theological point of view which was tempered with pragmatism, realization of the need for denominational unity, commitment to the church's missionary task, and impatience with precisionists. His membership on the Board of Directors of the Seminary enhanced his influence in leading to a reasonable resolution of the divergence that was afflicting the institution.

The resolution, which was adopted by the Assembly in 1929

and which created one board of trustees for Princeton Seminary, could not please everyone. The divergences of opinion on various theological issues were too wide. This fact was soon evident when Machen, who had been planning this move with the support of others, announced his resignation and intention to found a new Westminster Theological Seminary in Philadelphia. With him went Oswald T. Allis '05, Cornelius van Til '24, Robert Dick Wilson and a number of students from the Seminary in Princeton. Of the remaining faculty only two were present when Stevenson's successor took office in 1937. They were William Park Armstrong '97, and Frederick W. Loetscher '00. John D. Davis '83, had died in 1926, and Geerhardus Vos '85, in 1932. J. Ritchie Smith '76, had retired in 1929, Charles Erdman in 1936, and Caspar Wistar Hodge '01 in 1937.

As Lefferts A. Loetscher '28, son of Frederick W. Loetscher, has written—

The unfolding events had finally made mutually incompatible two tendencies which had existed side by side in the Princeton Theology from the beginning—a broad and warm evangelicalism on the one hand and a highly rational orthodoxy and extreme literalism on the other. It was best for both parts of the seminary's tradition that open bifurcation came at last, and that each could develop more fully and consistently its inherent implications unhampered by a really alien tendency. (Loetscher, *Broadening Church*, p. 147)

After reading this summary of the tumultuous events that transpired in the 1920s one may reasonably wonder how Princeton Theological Seminary could have continued to fulfill through all these years its assigned responsibilities of educating ministerial candidates. It did so, as the following account attests, but not without some distractions.

Faculty Appointments

One of the immediate effects of the controversies at Princeton Seminary was on the composition of the faculty. Between the time that Stevenson assumed the presidency in 1914 and the dissolution of the Board of Directors in 1929 only four new appointments were made: in 1914 J. Ritchie Smith '76, professor

J. Ross Stevenson, the Faculty and Members of Class of 1927

Second row (left to right): Caspar Wistar Hodge, Jr., William P. Armstrong, Geerhardu Vos, William B. Greene, Jr., President Stevenson, Robert Dick Wilson, Frederick W. Loetscher, J. Ritchie Smith, Charle B. Erdman; *Third row:* student, Donald Wheeler, William B. Sheddan, Osward T. Allis, J. Gresham Machen, Finley D. Jenkins, Joseph H Dulles, John H. Raven, Paul Martin, William P. McCulloch, student

of homiletics; in 1921 Finley D. Jenkins '19, instructor in systematic theology, and Donald Wheeler, instructor in elocution; and in 1928 Cornelius Van Til '24, instructor in apologetics who resigned with Machen the following year. As far as changes in personnel were concerned it had been a static faculty until death, resignations and retirements provided opportunities for the infusion of new blood that two decades earlier Woodrow Wilson had predicted would be needed.

In contrast to his first fifteen years as president, Stevenson was able to nominate between 1929 and his retirement in 1936

96

six men for election to the permanent faculty: Andrew W. Blackwood '08, Harold I. Donnelly '16, Henry S. Gehman, John E. Kuizenga, Donald MacKenzie, Edward H. Roberts '23, and Samuel M. Zwemer. Whereas each of these men then enjoyed and continue to be accorded respect for his academic contributions, the name of Roberts is the only one who has been memorialized in the name of a building on the campus a half century later. A dormitory bears the name of this professor who was successively registrar, dean of students, and Seminary dean. For twenty-two of those years he also served as secretary of the faculty, succeeding Paul Martin '86, who had been registrar and secretary of the faculty from 1906 to 1932.

As secretary of the faculty Roberts was subject to inspection of his minutes that first the directors and then the trustees continued to exercise over faculty records well into the 1930s. The directors assigned to its Committee on Examinations responsibility to report after monthly inspections by sub-committees how the faculty members organized their work and how they conducted their classes and examinations. All unsatisfactory students were to be referred to the directors who retained the prerogative to question any student who was eligible to take an examination.

Curricular Developments

It was during the first decade of the twentieth century that students, supported by the directors, had appealed for the inclusion in the curriculum of courses in the English Bible. The curriculum committee of the Board of Directors was also stressing the need for more attention to teaching of pastoral theology and ministerial responsibilities outside the pulpit. But even more disturbing to the professors was to them the amazingly disrespectful petition presented to the directors in 1909 by some students complaining about the teaching habits of several professors. This issue came before the board at the same meeting when its members were considering ways to stimulate more applications for admission. The previous year the faculty had reported to the directors that "Princeton's reputation for conservatism in Theology does not help her in this eastern region in these days when the predilection is for freer lines of thought. . . . in the west Princeton's well known Evangelical position is probably one of her best assets."

The concern of the directors was prompted by the junior class in 1908 which was the smallest since 1876. During Patton's presidency the enrollment varied between 150 and 192, averaging 170, the majority of whom were Presbyterians. In this period the Seminary was educating nearly one-fourth of all Presbyterian theological students in the country. Even with the reduction during World War I and the withdrawals of disaffected students in 1929 the enrollment during Stevenson's tenure averaged 198, including graduate students, and ranged between 114 and 255 during which period the maximum student housing accommodations on the campus were 250.

In the early 1920s the Seminary continued to enroll sons primarily of farmers, mechanics, merchants and naturally ministers; in other words, primarily from working class families. This was at a time when the enrollment of foreign students from China, Japan, and even Great Britain was being limited by the post World War I stricter immigration laws. Although at that time forty percent of the students were members of other denominations than Presbyterian the enrollment was being hampered by requirements of some denominations that their ministerial candidates attend their own denominational seminaries. In addition to these factors, according to a report of President Stevenson, active propaganda to encourage attendance at other Presbyterian seminaries was disseminated at a conference of Presbyterian students in May 1924 because of the conservative theology taught at Princeton where the conference was being held.

In 1934 Stevenson reported that the size of the faculty was the same as when he assumed the presidency, and that with the exception of the addition of Christian education the basic course offerings had undergone few changes during his tenure, but that the curriculum was better balanced. The previous year the trustees' curriculum committee had recommended the introduction of conference, discussion and seminar teaching with less reliance on lectures, noting at the same time that these innovations would require more faculty personnel and a reorganized curriculum. Additional faculty was obviously not possible at a time when salaries had been reduced fifteen percent during the great depression.

In 1914, when Stevenson was assuming the presidency, an increased number of electives was added to the curriculum over the stiff opposition of Benjamin Warfield. These included courses available at the University where qualified seminary students could also earn a master's degree. Because of this inter-institutional curricular exchange it was necessary for the Seminary to conform to the revised academic schedule adopted by the University in 1916. Despite this introduction of a new academic calendar, not until 1923 was the academic year of the Seminary divided into two semesters with a mandatory reduction in the number of subjects in which a student could be enrolled at one time. Prior to that revision some students were enrolled in as many as twelve courses simultaneously throughout the year.

In 1921 the influential Professor Warfield died leaving a legacy of some 2,700 Princeton Seminary students who had studied theology under his tutelage; he also bequeathed an endowment for the Annie Kinkead Warfield lectureship, named for his invalid wife. His penetrating influence was not able, however, to prevent an increase in elective options. In that year the catalogue listed eighty-six courses offered in eight departments: Old Testament, New Testament, Semitic philology, church history, apologetics and Christian ethics, systematic theology, practical theology and homiletics, and history of religion and missions. Classes were then held in the mornings, including Saturdays, starting at 8:10, as well as late afternoons, and three evenings each week. By 1931 mid-year examinations were introduced, all courses were offered as three-credit hour minimum, and the previous eight departments were consolidated into five.

Following enactment by the State of enabling legislation, the Seminary awarded in 1922 its first Bachelor of Theology degrees in place of certificates of graduation to those completing the three year course of study. During the previous two decades degrees had been awarded only to those few students who had successfully completed their undergraduate and seminary studies and who had pursued an additional year at the Seminary. In the early 1920s for the first time a course of study leading to a master's degree was introduced.

Other Educational Developments

In recognition of the importance of competence in public speaking on the part of the clergy, Donald Wheeler, a master at the nearby Lawrenceville School, was appointed in 1924 to be the instructor in elocution, as previously noted, and remained on the faculty of the Seminary until his retirement as professor in 1953. It was also in 1926 that the trustees appropriated $1,100 to support the chapel choir and the employment of a "musical trainer." Three years later the appointment of the first director of music was made, preceding by several years the arrival of the Westminster Choir College to Princeton.

In 1931 members of the choir and staff of Westminster, then located in Ithaca, New York, visited the campus and made such a favorable impression that seminary students responded with increased interest in church music and officials of the Seminary encouraged a transfer of the College to Princeton, a move that was accomplished the next year. Following an agreement in which the Seminary made certain commitments (in effect until 1991 when the College negotiated with the Seminary so that it might effect a merger with Rider College), Mrs. J. Livingston (Sophia Strong) Taylor of Cleveland provided funds to purchase the land and construct the first four of the Choir College's new buildings. With an enrollment of approximately 120 students and a dozen faculty members this new addition to the educational institutions in Princeton brought innumerable cultural benefits to the community. It also provided two successive directors of music at the Seminary: John Finley Williamson, administrative director of the Choir College, who served for two years, 1932 to 1934, followed by David Hugh Jones who retired as professor of music in 1970 after adding significantly to the appreciation and knowledge of music on the part of several generations of Seminary students.

Just as the presence in Princeton of Westminster Choir College was partially the result of encouragement from the Seminary, more than a century earlier the Seminary was located in Princeton following a wooing by the College of New Jersey. The relationship of these latter two institutions, extending well over a century, became the subject of a joint review in the early 1930s when a professor at the Seminary had assumed that the policy of free tuition in the University for sons of Seminary faculty was still in force even though it had been discontinued two years earlier.

For many years the University had maintained a policy of providing financial assistance to the sons of ministers. In 1921 the University extended this policy by providing free tuition to the sons of the Seminary faculty. During the stringencies of the deep depression this policy was rescinded in 1932, and seminary sons were encouraged to file regular applications for scholarship grants. It was this revision that prompted the joint review by the two boards of trustees.

Since the founding of the Seminary in 1812 there had been friendly communication between the institutions and their respective faculties. There had been mutual use of libraries, reciprocal use of buildings, and exchange of land when the University in 1914 built the Graduate College which was initially heated by the nearby Seminary power plant. The Seminary contributed to the cost of constructing the second infirmary at the University in 1924 and made annual payments for health services which were provided to Seminary students. And, when the enrollment at the Seminary was reduced in some years, it provided room accommodations for a few students from the University to the mutual benefit of both institutions. All of these factors and the historically friendly relations between the institutions were recounted, and further agreements were reached at the time of the review that facilitated the continued enrollment of qualified Seminary students in graduate studies at the University. But unfortunately the great disruption at the Seminary during the remainder of that decade, as well as other unrelated factors, adversely affected the inter-institutional personal relationships which subsequently were never again as intimate.

In 1929, because of financial pressures, one other educational enterprise at the Seminary was terminated. This was the *Princeton Theological Review*, a successor to the *Biblical Repertory*, started by Charles Hodge over a century earlier. By 1890, when Benjamin Warfield became editor, it was known as the *Presbyterian and Reformed Review* and then in 1903 adopted the name by which it was identified when the trustees discontinued the annual subsidization of $3,000 and recommended to the faculty editors that it cease publication which it did for a period of some years. This $3,000 was relatively a small item compared to the much larger and persistent financial concerns that confronted the Seminary through most of the first third of the twentieth century.

Continued Financial Concerns

Shortly after Patton was inaugurated as the first president financial conditions suddenly appeared very auspicious for the Seminary—at least for a short time. In 1903 a special meeting of the trustees was convened to consider the largest bequest that had been received to that date. Mrs. Mary J. Winthrop of New York, who had earlier been a generous donor, had left part of her estate to the Seminary and established the Gelston-Winthrop Fund, named for her sister and herself, which when the will was settled amounted to over $1.6 million. A year after Mrs. Winthrop's death the Charles T. Haley professorship was established by a gift of $90,000 from his sister. These two donations, especially the former, permitted the appointment of several teaching assistants, the creation of the position of registrar, and some curricular rearrangements.

In a spirit of modest euphoria the directors in the fall of 1905 proposed that the yearly salaries of all professors be raised from $3,700 to $5,000, and then reality forced reconsideration two months later when the increase was reduced to $4,500. The previous year had ended with a deficit of $14,000, and in 1905 there were no recorded gifts for the first time in many years. The following year caused even greater concern when it was discovered, following the apparent self-imposed death of Frank K. Hipple, a trustee since 1895, that he had appropriated Seminary funds for his own benefit as well as funds of the General Assembly for which he served as treasurer. Fortunately, after the settlement of his affairs, the loss to the Seminary was less than $2,000 and the year 1907 ended with an operating surplus of nearly $8,000, but deficits soon reappeared. Successive years of insufficient financing with deficits averaging $6,500 forced the boards in 1910 to recognize that there was need to raise a half million dollars. The only immediate financial improvement was receipt the following year of a bequest of $76,000 for scholarships from Mrs. James Reid Hay of Philadelphia in memory of her husband. Even though deficits continued to plague the Seminary at the time of Patton's retirement, the institution's total assets, including investments and property, amounted to nearly $4 million in 1912.

When Stevenson accepted the presidency in 1914 he was aware of the conservative stance of a majority of the faculty and of the need to raise funds to stem the frequent deficits with which the institution was annually afflicted. On the other hand, he could not have anticipated the turbulence that prevailed during his twenty-two year tenure. First a world war with all its disruptions, then almost a decade of denominational discord and personal conflicts in the Seminary, followed by a deep economic depression that affected all of society. During each of these calamitous events endeavors were made to strengthen the financial conditions of the Seminary and its staff—not always successfully.

Initiation of a pension plan for the faculty was abandoned in 1915 when the finance committee of the Board of Directors concluded "that in view of the substantial salaries paid to the Professors, together with free house rent, there is not the need for such retiring allowances as is existent in other institutions where the emoluments are on a much lower scale." At that time Princeton was the largest seminary in the country and had one of the largest endowments, if not the largest.

After World War I faculty salaries were increased by twenty percent on the basis of pledges from five trustees to meet the additional costs for one year. At the same time the trustees calculated the financial needs of the Seminary to be more than $4.3 million, one half of which they concluded should be raised immediately. By now budgets were running more than $200,000 each year and deficits were as high as $16,000. A campaign was undertaken that raised some $600,000, more than half of which was in tentative promises. There were, however, several substantial gifts received in the early 1920s.

John T. Monsen of New Haven, Connecticut, bequeathed $125,000, the income of which was to be applied to operating expenses. Henry H. Laughlin of Philadelphia established a $100,000 memorial in recognition of his son, Edward Reed Laughlin '98. And Thomas W. Synnott contributed $75,000, supplemented five years later by a professorship in Christian education. Synnott had been a member of the Board of Trustees since 1898 and was president during the turbulent era from 1912 to 1930.

Despite these financial accomplishments special committees of the two boards reported in 1921 that the general reaction of potential donors in the post war period was not conducive to giving, and that "the very traits of character, habits of thought and fundamentals of faith that tie them to a conservative institution, make them cautious in the matter of making pledges to any cause. . . . The immediate future holds little hope for large subscriptions." By 1922 the contingency funds had been exhausted, the costs of the endowment campaign had to be charged against general expenses, and to meet the operating budget the endowment fund had to be employed. By 1924 Stevenson emphasized to the boards that while the Seminary was over-all a prosperous institution it was necessary that the trustees, directors and faculty cooperate in the development of a coordinated financial plan. He noted the need of a pension plan for the faculty who repeatedly emphasized the importance of a common dining hall while the trustees supported an addition to the library.

With the turmoil that was brewing in the Seminary during

this period there was no likelihood that the three bodies could develop a plan for any coordinated effort. This had to await the formation of the new, single Board of Trustees in 1930 which estimated the financial needs to be $1 million for the chapel, a dining hall, new power plant, larger faculty, pensions and scholarships. With the onset of the depression only one of these goals was attainable. In fact, income from investments soon fell, mortgages were in default, faculty salaries were reduced by fifteen percent, charges to students for heat and light were doubled to $24 a year, various plant maintenance was deferred, the size of scholarships was reduced, and unemployment among the clergy was increasing. Even though on occasion the Seminary had to borrow funds from banks to meet its payroll, it had finally introduced a pension plan that increased its budget initially during this period by $12,000 a year.

With these prevailing conditions of continuous frustration that existed over more than two decades it is gratifying to note that at least one new building was constructed on the Seminary campus during the Stevenson administration.

Physical Facilities

The one building in whose cornerstone laying President Stevenson was able to participate was Payne Hall. The ceremony occurred in the fall of 1921 after six years of discussion and planning in which the faculty, directors and trustees all agreed that there needed to be an apartment house where missionaries and their families could reside while on furlough. Professor and Mrs. Erdman purchased and donated the land located on Alexander Street near the campus; James H. Post, a trustee from 1908 to 1937, procured two adjoining properties for the Seminary; and Mr. and Mrs. Calvin N. Payne contributed over $140,000 to pay for the cost and interior decorations of the building that was designed by Arthur H. Brockie of Philadelphia. Mr. Payne had been engaged in the petroleum business in Titusville, Pennsylvania, where the first well to produce oil had been sunk in 1859. On his death in 1926 he left an endowment for maintenance of the building amounting to $100,000.

The only other major edifice that was built by the Seminary in the early part of the twentieth century was a coal fired electric and heating plant, constructed in 1908 at a cost of $76,000, two-thirds of which was financed through bonds. The costs were amortized by charges initially of $12 a year to each student who enjoyed warmer rooms and hotter water, and at the same time the cost for the Seminary to produce these services was reduced. All coal stoves and kerosene lamps had by then been totally replaced. As Andrew W. Blackwood '08 recounted "each room was lighted by a small bulb, ingeniously put into sockets by a locking mechanism that prevented bulb-snatching. When lighted, the bulb looked like a hot nail in a bottle." (PTS *Alumni News*, Summer 1980, pp. 2–5) Shortly thereafter new plumbing and toilet facilities, including drinking fountains and popular shower baths, were installed in all three dormitories. Of significant importance was the installation in 1909 of a ladies' toilet on the second floor of Alexander Hall. Several years later a fire in this historic building required the recasting of a new bell to replace the one that had called students and faculty to classes since 1828.

The election of the first president of the Seminary in 1902 must have been at least a partial catalyst to stimulate both students and faculty to call attention to their desires for improved physical facilities. The students petitioned for a gymnasium, and the faculty proposed improvements in Miller Chapel and the installation of a modern, full-sized, rich-toned organ. The first request was addressed by the trustees in 1910 when they authorized that the former refectory, which had recently been used as a dormitory, be converted to a gymnasium. Athletic equipment was installed and additional land was acquired where students could engage in outdoor sports. This arrangement was not altered until 1929 when two rooms in the western end of the gymnasium were reassigned as the president's offices, the precursor to it becoming the Administration Building in 1945.

Also in 1910 the trustees responded to the faculty's proposal with respect to Miller Chapel, but on a much more modest scale by the purchase of a two-manual pipe organ at a cost of $1500. This instrument served until 1933 when a major move was undertaken. In fact, the entire structure was moved from behind the east end of Alexander Hall to a more central and prominent place on the campus; the building was enlarged; and the organ owned by Mrs. J. Livingston Taylor, the benefactor of Westminster Choir College, was moved from her home in Cleveland, largely at her expense, and installed as a replacement in Miller Chapel.

With the advent of a president in 1902 a domicile was required. After some renovations the recently purchased house at 86 Mercer Street served admirably as the home for the president. Springdale, as it was and has been known, was built in 1846 for Richard Stockton, a seventh generation Stockton in America. At the time of purchase by the Seminary, Springdale was owned by Bayard Stockton. At one time it had been occupied as a girls' boarding school. Here Patton and each of his successors and their families have resided.

With the addition of Payne Hall there were ten main buildings on the campus: chapel, recitation hall, gymnasium, three dormitories, power plant, and two libraries, in addition to eleven residences adjacent to the campus. To maintain these buildings almost an entire new staff of janitors had to be appointed following World War I when five men, whose average length of service was thirty-four years, either retired or died. Their individual length of appointment could not, however, equal the forty-five years that Joseph H. Dulles '77 served as the Seminary librarian, in addition to his various other concurrently performed administrative duties.

Both the directors and trustees, as well as the faculty, maintained a special interest in the library. By the early 1900s the two buildings, one designated for reference and the other for circulation, were beginning to be inadequate to house the collection of books, pamphlets, and other items that was growing each year. With the installation of electric lighting the buildings were open longer hours and the staff had to be increased. By 1913, when there were nearly 100,000 volumes, consideration was given to the alternative of building an addition to the New Lenox, the brick building, or replacing it at a cost of $500,000. The former choice was selected and the work completed in 1925 at a cost of $47,000 with anticipation that the needs for book space would be sufficient for the next twenty-five years.

Whereas only twelve years elapsed between the initiation of formal consideration of an addition to the library and its actual completion, a half century of appeals, talk, planning and fund raising were required before a replacement to the old refectory could be erected. After frequent mention of the unsatisfactory club situation by the faculty in their annual reports, the directors in 1913 authorized that architectural plans be drawn for a building which was estimated to cost as much as $75,000. By 1930 when a central dining hall had not been built the *Princeton Seminary Bulletin* reported that the clubs then in existence were facing difficulties both in finding suitable facilities that could be rented at reasonable rates, and in providing nourishing and appetizing meals without increasing charges. The report further noted that these pressures will increase whenever the enrollment of the Seminary expands. Despite these difficulties students generally relished the comradeship and friendships that were made through their club associations, a nostalgic remembrance that alumni retained long after the Mackay Campus Center was finally completed in 1952.

Campus Life

In order to inform its alumni and friends that the Seminary was functioning well after the divisiveness of the 1920s, the *Princeton Seminary Bulletin* included in its November 1934 issue a series of articles portraying in a restrained manner many of the favorable features of campus life that were being maintained as of old. One of these articles was written by Wilson Bennett '34 in which he described student life at the Seminary. From this and other descriptions a gradually changing picture emerges for the first four decades of the twentieth century.

In the 1930s and 1940s each student was a member of one of the four student-operated clubs (Benham, Calvin, Friars and Warfield) to which at the time of commencement alumni would joyously return to associate and reminisce with their fellow club members. All three daily meals were served in these clubs interspersed with special occasions such as birthdays or engagement announcements when the "culprit" was expected to provide a special treat such as pie or ice cream. At one period the Seminary sponsored a club, unsuccessfully at first, in the University dining halls and then in a nearby family house, and at about the same time provided a small annual subsidy to the clubs to help them meet their increasing costs.

Although some students were married, for which they were urged to obtain approval from the Seminary, they ran the risk of losing scholarship aid since it was assumed that if a student could afford to be married he had less financial need. Most students, both Presbyterian and non-Presbyterian, received some form of financial aid even though the total estimated costs were less than $300, having risen over the years from $175 in 1908. Tuition charges had not yet been instituted. To meet expenses many students worked part-time in various capacities including assignments in nearby parishes. These responsibilities affected both class attendance and appearance in the Sunday morning chapel services, especially when students began to own their personal automobiles. Because of congestion, by the 1930s special restrictions had to be enforced with respect to parking on the campus.

After the chapel building was relocated, attendance at the Sunday services did improve temporarily but in time the faculty and trustees recognized that many students preferred to attend local parishes in the area either as individual communicants, parish assistants, or in deputations at organized religious meetings. As in the past, prayer sessions led by faculty and students were held each week-day morning, each club and each class conducted prayer sessions, and the tradition of a monthly evening session devoted to missions was continued. Throughout the academic year there were many occasions to hear visiting lectures and preachers.

Irregular appearance at class sessions was another matter. At various times, because of irregular attendance, the faculty was forced to remind students of the declaration to which each had subscribed at the time of his matriculation and which for many years was printed in the catalogue.

Deeply impressed with the sense of the importance of improving in knowledge, prudence and piety, in my preparation for the Gospel ministry, I solemnly promise, in a reliance on divine grace, that I will faithfully and diligently attend on all instructions of this Seminary, and that I will conscientiously and vigilantly observe all the rules and regulations specified in the Plan [of the Seminary] for its instruction and government, so far as the same relates to the students; and that I will obey all the lawful requisitions, and readily yield to all the wholesome admonitions of the professors and directors of the Seminary while I shall continue a member of it.

When the converted gymnasium was opened in 1910 it provided space and facilities for basketball, boxing, gymnastics, wrestling as well as a music and social room. But what appealed even more to some was the "splendid bathing facilities." The *Princeton Seminary Bulletin* at that time expressed the hope "that this finely equipped gymnasium will attract not only the strong, robust men in the Seminary, but that it will prove to be a blessing to students who are inclined to be weak, anaemic or nervous, and by whom gymnasium work should be regarded not only as a privilege, but a sacred duty." At various times other informal and intramural sports were pursued that included baseball, cricket, rugby, and soccer, some jointly with undergraduate and graduate men at the University. In at least one year home and home basketball games were played against Union Seminary in New York.

The health of the students was generally quite good, although there were deaths that did occur. In 1910, an exceptional year, three students died, one from poliomyelitis, one from meningitis, and a Ceylonese (Sri Lankan) from drowning. The death of a foreign student was always an especially poignant occasion. In the few instances in which this occurred there were no family or personal funds available. Samuel Atanasov, a Bulgarian member of the class of '31, died in 1930 within a few days of the onset of his illness and was buried in the Princeton Cemetery. The good health of most of the students was attributed not only to their age but also to the care provided by the

Seminary with the assistance of the University. Beginning in 1920 William G. Schauffer, a local physician, administered individual physical examinations and gave lectures on personal hygiene to the students, services that he provided until he was succeeded a half dozen years later by Van M. Ellis and in 1936 by John R. Burbidge.

The student activity that was probably more widely known was the singing group that began as the Seminary Chorus in 1923 with twenty-eight voices under the direction of Finley D. Jenkins '19, an instructor at the Seminary from 1921 until 1929 when he retired because of deteriorating health. The Chorus presented concerts not only locally but also in New York and Philadelphia. Commencing in the 1930s the presence of Westminster Choir College stimulated further interest in music and helped to lay the foundation for subsequent Seminary choirs that traveled more widely to present concerts in churches at the request of numerous alumni.

Support of and by Alumni

Unless one was granted an honorary status, one was required at least to have been admitted and to have matriculated in order to be considered to be an alumna or an alumnus of the Seminary. In the early 1930s two policy decisions regarding admissions were made that affected matriculation and in turn membership in the alumni body.

The first of these decisions was applied to students entering in 1934 when growing numbers of ministers were unemployed and the placement of graduates became increasingly difficult. In that year for the first time the Seminary instituted a policy of screening more carefully those seeking admission and insisting that those who were admitted meet minimum standards. As a result forty-five were denied admission and the academic standards began to rise as did coincidentally the proportion of Presbyterian students which had been only fifty-four percent five years earlier.

The second policy change had occurred in 1928 when the first female degree candidate was granted admission. Muriel van

Orden Jennings, a graduate of Radcliffe College, became the first alumna to be graduated from Princeton Seminary when in 1932 she received both her bachelor and master of theology degrees. She had been preceded, however, by two other women who had been enrolled as part-time students: Margaret Baldwin Stoner in 1917 who had previously studied at Ohio Wesleyan University, and Elizabeth Helen Graf in the class of 1924, who was a graduate of the University of Pennsylvania in 1920.

In 1933 the first *Biographical Catalogue* of alumni was compiled and reported that since its founding in 1812 the Seminary had matriculated 7,729 individuals of whom 6,065 were pastors, 561 missionaries, 317 professors, 399 in other educational pursuits, 327 laymen, and sixty unidentified. Eighty-six percent were Presbyterians and there had been 641 students from thirty-nine countries. Of the total alumni 3,662 were then living.

Of the foreign students during the first decades of the twentieth century the largest number were from Japan, the first of whom to receive a degree from the Seminary was Chojuro Aoki '01 who later devoted his life to teaching in his native land. Among the other relatively numerous Japanese students at Princeton was Toyohiko Kagawa '15, who became the internationally famous evangelist and social worker.

Of the American nationals, who were graduated between 1912 and 1935, fourteen percent became missionaries. While the largest numbers of missionary graduates went to China, India and Korea, others assumed missionary assignments on all of the continents. This surge of missionary zeal predated the change after World War II when other world religions experienced a period of revitalization and when Christian churches in other lands sought to be recognized as peers in the ecumenical movement.

Fortunately for the community of Princeton the Witherspoon Street Presbyterian Church, among whose founders was Betsey Stockton, enjoyed as its pastors between 1901 and 1929 three successive black graduates who later attained positions of wide influence. Leonard Z. Johnson '03 became a professor at Howard University; George S. Stark '02 was for many years pastor of the Siloam Church in Brooklyn; and Augusts E. Bennett '20 filled several pastorates, including Grace Church in Chicago where he was also Moderator of that Presbytery.

Maintaining an interest in its graduates, the largest body of alumni of any theological school, Princeton Seminary encouraged its alumni to return to the campus both for personal pleasure and intellectual renewal. At the time of commencement in June 1930, following the organization of the revised Board of Trustees earlier that year, over four hundred attended the annual meeting of the Alumni Association when a new plan was adopted which stated "The *purpose* of this Association shall be to co-operate with the Board of Trustees and the Faculty in the support and advancement of the interests of the Seminary." For some years the graduation exercises had been held in the First Presbyterian Church, then moved because of space requirements to Princeton University's Alexander Hall, before being transferred to the University Chapel where they have subsequently been conducted.

In addition to the alumni gathering in June the Alumni Association with support from the Seminary sponsored conferences of several days in the fall which alumni were invited to attend at nominal cost and hear lectures by faculty and invited speakers who also led discussion groups on topics of intellectual and practical concern to ministers.

End of an Era

With the retirement of J. Ross Stevenson because of age, the end of a tumultuous epoch in the history of Princeton Theological Seminary had arrived. In retrospect one may conjecture that, partially as a result of the friction that was engendered by the deep theological division which split the Church, his contributions to the Seminary have not been fully appreciated. Accusations that he was a church politician have been made by individuals who apparently discounted the need for leaders who have the wisdom and grace to know when and how to compromise constructively.

Stevenson recognized that economic and social conditions

had changed and were continuing to change, and that to continue to be a positive force in society Princeton Seminary had to prepare future clergy to minister to the members of this new society. Through war, through economic depression, and through what was an inevitable theological conflict, Stevenson ultimately led the Seminary during an extended period of much agony and pain on a reoriented course that it has pursued during the rest of the century. His successor arrived in 1936 with innumerable problems to resolve but also an opportunity to build in a way that Stevenson was never permitted to enjoy.

6

The Burden of the Word

MALACHI

If it were not for three native-born Presbyterian clergymen of the early nineteenth century—Archibald Alexander, Ashbel Green and Samuel Miller—the founding of Princeton Theological Seminary in 1812 might never have occurred. Their contributions have been indelibly written in the pages of history. Similarly, if it were not for three Scotsmen neither the Seminary nor Princeton University would have attained the reputations that each enjoys in this last decade of the twentieth century.

Having elected five presidents in a period of less than twenty years, the trustees of the College of New Jersey in 1766 faced the daunting task of selecting a successor to Samuel Finley who had died in office, as had each of his predecessors. The task was daunting because the contentious New Siders and Old Siders were each advocating their respective candidates to direct this new and somewhat fragile college in the direction of their theological convictions. In a most fortunate solution to their dilemma the trustees looked to Paisley, Scotland, and elected the ordained clergyman, John Witherspoon, who among his many attributes was not involved in the colonial Presbyterian disputes that prevailed at the time. Under his leadership the College thrived and produced many of the leaders of the emerging nation, as well as clergy of both the New Side and Old Side factions.

Exactly a century later the trustees of the College were again faced with the task of selecting a president as the schism between the Old School and New School Presbyterians was about to be resolved. On this occasion they elected the conservative Professor William Henry Green of the Seminary. Following his declination the trustees followed the example of their predecessors and turned again to Scotland. James McCosh, a native of Ayrshire, came to Princeton from a professorship at Queen's College in Belfast, Ireland. It was the influence of this minister of the Free Church of Scotland that laid the basis for the eventual transformation of this sectarian college into a university with its current pre-eminent reputation.

Similarly, at a time of healing following the deep division of the 1920s between the Presbyterian conservatives and modernists, the trustees of the Seminary with what proved to be great wisdom elected in 1936 John A. Mackay, a native of Inverness, Scotland, to be the institution's third president. At that time through a combination of circumstances, some fortunate and some not so fortunate, the Seminary was in need of the type of conciliatory and ecumenical leadership that Mackay had pursued in his missionary assignments. Under his tutelage the Seminary was able to thrive as it expanded and strengthened its educational offerings for students in its various degree programs, and through continuing education courses for the ordained clergy. Just as his Scottish predecessors had reinvigorated the College of New Jersey—Witherspoon in the eighteenth century, McCosh in the nineteenth century—Mackay brought an invigoration in the twentieth century to the Seminary which now serves all Presbyterians, as well as many other denominations. To these three Scots the educational institutions in Princeton will be in their debt forever.

A Gentle Breeze

John Alexander Mackay was born in 1889 and educated at Aberdeen University before entering Princeton Seminary from which he was graduated in 1915. His academic accomplishments qualified him for a Gelston-Winthrop fellowship that permitted him to study in Madrid, Spain, for a year before he married and with his wife undertook missionary assignments in South America. There they founded and conducted a school while at the same time he earned a doctoral degree at San Marcos University in Lima, Peru, the first university to be established in the western hemisphere. There as a professor he sub-

John A. Mackay
President of the Seminary from 1936 to 1959
and his wife, Jane Wells Mackay

sequently taught and as a representative of the Federation of
Young Men's Christian Associations lectured throughout
South America until 1932 when Robert Elliott Speer induced
him to move to New York and join the staff of the Presbyterian
Board of Foreign Missions. In his new position he had respon-
sibilities for the Church's missionary activities in Africa and
South America. Again it was Robert Speer who prevailed on
Mackay to accept the presidency of Princeton Theological Sem-
inary in 1936.

Writing in the *Princeton Seminary Bulletin* twenty-three
years later, at the time of Mackay's retirement, Henry S. Gehman, who had been appointed to the faculty in 1930, described
the transformation that occurred at the Seminary during this
new administration.

Princeton Theological Seminary had made the transition from the old
to the new. It was no longer content to remain on the defensive or to
perpetuate traditional knowledge, but it burst forth with a new energy

and aggressive spirit. Without discarding its enduring achievements of the past it began to blaze a path into the future and to make a more vital contribution to the life of the Church. It was as though a gentle breeze had begun to blow through the institution, and the writer felt a freedom in his teaching that he had never experienced before.

Mackay commanded respect. He was dignified in his manner, impressive as he conducted religious services or spoke in public, usually without notes. He was also gracious and thoughtful, and a gentleman of wide learning filled with a quiet ecumenical zeal that was evident in the transformation of the Seminary during his presidency. Despite his force of personality and his penchant for checking each detail on the campus, he more often inspired others with his conceptual ideas and reflections frequently expressed in metaphors. Years later he has been repeatedly quoted for his "Balcony and the Road," in which the balcony represented spectators who sit and philosophize, and the road was where life is lived with all its tensions and strife, and where choices have to be made and decisions implemented. Mackay was a man whose head could be on the balcony but whose feet and actions were on the road.

A year after his arrival Mackay outlined in the November 1937 issue of the *Princeton Seminary Bulletin* the basis of his educational philosophy.

The primary and most important function of a theological seminary is to prepare heralds of the Gospel and shepherds of the soul. This function is worthily discharged when the Seminary makes adequate provision for the progress of its students in learning and piety. . . .

A strong graduate school of Reformed theology at Princeton is imperatively needed. The renaissance of evangelical learning which has flushed the horizon of European thought must come to America. Certain false conceptions regarding the Reformed faith which have been devastating in their influence must be dissipated. Our Seminary must seize the present providential opportunity to give vital theological leadership in our Church, our country, and the world of today.

Mackay was committed to the education and preparation of Christian preachers, Christian scholars, Christian teachers, and Christian statesmen in the environment of an ecumenical campus community. He insisted that no theological tests should be applied in admission of students to what he insisted should be an inclusive seminary in an integral relationship with an inclusive denomination. Throughout his life Mackay was a conservative Scottish Presbyterian who recognized that Christianity enjoyed a rich ecclesiastical and theological heritage that should be recognized in a spirit of Christian togetherness. As one of his successors, Thomas W. Gillespie '54, stated years later, "His was not a *new theology*, but theology *in a new key*." (*PS Bulletin*, #3, 1989)

Rebuilding the Faculty

Of the many tasks facing the new president in 1936 none was more important than the appointment of new members of the faculty, which was being depleted by retirements and deaths. Within one year of his arrival Charles R. Erdman and Samuel M. Zwemer retired, and Harold I. Donnelly and Caspar Wistar Hodge, Jr. died. Mackay's first professorial appointments were Elmer G. Homrighausen '24 and Otto A. Piper from Germany, individuals whom several generations of seminarians have recalled with respect and appreciation. Within a few years other appointments followed. Among them were alumni, non-alumni, foreign born, and native born, a diverse group of men who met Mackay's inseparably bound requirements of Christian commitment and academic accomplishment.

Additions to the faculty in the 1940s were in chronological order: Hugh T. Kerr, Jr., Bruce M. Metzger '38, Lefferts A. Loetscher '28, Charles T. Fritsch '35, Edward J. Jurji '42, a native of Syria, Howard T. Kuist, J. Donald Butler, and Norman V. Hope from Scotland. In 1947 four additional appointments were made: Georges A. Barrois '42 and Emile Caillet both born in France, Paul L. Lehmann, and Donald MacLeod '46, the latter born in Canada. At the end of the decade George S. Hendry, a Scot, was added to the group of foreign born faculty members. Before Mackay's retirement five additional professors were appointed, all in the 1950s: W. J. Beeners '48; D. Campbell Wyckoff; James W. Clarke, another Scot; Edward A. Dowey '43, Samuel W. Blizzard '39, and John H. Hick, an Englishman.

John A. Mackay and Members of the Faculty and Administration, 1958-1959

First row (left to right): K. S. Gapp, J. C. Wilson, G. S. Hendry,
J. W. Clarke, H. T. Kuist, E. G. Homrighausen, President Mackay,
O. A. Piper, N. V. Hope, D. H. Jones, E. Cailliet, H. T. Kerr, Jr.,
D. C. Wyckoff; *second row*: J. MacCarroll, C. T. Fritsch,
E. Hatfield, E. J. Jurji, E. A. Dowey, Jr., J. H. Smylie, W. J. Beeners,
H. H. Cox, L. A. Loetscher, C. A. Yang, D. Macleod, J. P. Martin,
G. A. Barrois; *third row*: O. C. Hopper, J. F. Armstrong,
H. C. Prichard, S. W. Blizzard, T. G. Belote, C. H. Massa,
D. M. Stine, R. E. Sanders, D. E. Bussis, A. P. Dohrenburg,
A. D. Duba; *fourth row*: G. W. Loos, Jr., V. M. Rogers,
J. E. Smylie, R. M. Hoag, E. S. Golden, W. G. Bodamer,
R. W. Lyon, W. Brower

This was an admirable group of men, all of whom enhanced the reputation of Princeton Seminary with their academic accomplishments, teaching competencies, and relatively harmonious relationships. Whereas many of them were known internationally through their writings as well as their attendance at gatherings and meetings in foreign lands, all of them rekindled memories for many years among the widespread Seminary alumni. In 1937 Mackay proposed the creation of the first professorship in ecumenics and a year later was appointed to fill that chair.

During the early months of his administration Mackay had appointed several visiting professors who replaced temporarily those who had retired or died. Among these were Emil Brunner from Switzerland and Joseph L. Hromadka from Czechoslovakia, both internationally known theologians whose appointments were made possible as a result of the social disruptions in Europe following the rise to power of the Nazis in Germany. These appointments elicited objections, however, from several faculty members and at least one trustee, to which Mackay responded that not merely the Seminary but the entire Presbyterian Church in the United States of America gained by the intellectual infusion that these able men brought to the campus. This was a time when Princeton Seminary was receptive to the teachings of Karl Barth and when the campus was experiencing, as it did especially in the 1940s and 1950s, the gentle breeze of liberation and ecumenical awareness. To permit an even wider choice of potential faculty members a few years later the General Assembly approved further changes in the plan for the Seminary that permitted the appointment of lay Presbyterians to the faculty.

By the end of Mackay's tenure the faculty, including all ranks both full-time and part-time, had been increased to sixty-four. With the exception of Henry Gehman all had been appointed during his presidency. This notable increase was necessitated by the demands of a larger student enrollment, an expansion in the course offerings, and the establishment and re-establishment of various academic activities.

Academic Enrichment

Pursuing his commitment to a doctoral program in theology Mackay obtained approval in 1940 for the establishment of a program leading to the degree of doctor of theology with the first degree awarded in 1944 to Donald M. Davies '40. By 1942 the program had enrolled eighteen students and, despite the war years, had become an important academic activity of the Seminary. This was not, however, the only development that was occurring on the Princeton campus in this period of stimulating academic growth.

The idea of reestablishing a summer school, which had existed briefly prior to World War I, was revived. This led to discussions with the Alumni Association regarding the holding of a ministers' conference the final week in June of 1938. From this beginning the Institute of Theology was established in 1942 with a highly concentrated ten-day program of serious theological study and reflection. Led by members of the faculty and complemented by visiting lecturers the Institute has continued for more than half a century to attract a yearly attendance of several hundred clergy and lay persons representing in a typical year as many as thirty denominations from a half dozen countries and some two dozen states.

While the Institute was being developed the Seminary was engaged in discussions that would lead to its involvement in Christian education. In 1941 the General Assembly had recommended that colleges of Christian education be associated with seminaries. This action prompted the Tennent College of Christian Education in Philadelphia, the successor to the Philadelphia School for Christian Workers founded in 1907, to initiate discussions with Princeton Seminary with which it soon agreed to merge in 1944. Concurrent with this development the buildings of the Hun School, located two blocks from the Seminary, became available for purchase and here the Seminary inaugurated its three-year course leading to the degree of Master in Religious Education. During its first five years the program enrolled seventy students, sixty-five of whom were women preparing to become assistants to ministers and to fill other positions that were then open to women. This was several years before the Presbyterian Church removed its restrictions in 1956 that had limited ordination to men.

Under the direction of J. Donald Butler the new program in Christian education was incorporated into the Seminary curriculum that by 1940 had been reorganized into four departments of Biblical literature, history, systematic theology, and practical theology with a total offering of nearly one hundred courses. By 1957 when the recording of class attendance was discontinued, the number of courses, including those offered in alternate years, had been increased more than two and one half times. If this large increase had been instituted in the early 1940s, the inauguration of an accelerated program with three terms a year to meet the demands of the military requirements during World War II would have been more difficult to manage. In 1944 the Navy inaugurated its V-12(s) program to train military chaplains, but with the end of the war in 1945 it and the accelerated program were discontinued within two years.

In spite of the disruptions that were entailed in transforming the campus operations during those war years, the degree of Bachelor of Theology that had been conferred by the Seminary since 1921 was replaced in 1944 by the Bachelor of Divinity, which in turn was supplanted by the Master of Divinity in 1971. Concurrent with this change in 1944 fewer courses were prescribed and more electives were permitted to meet the requirements for graduation. Among the new electives that indicated an expanding horizon for those entering religious vocations were such courses as cultural anthropology, child development, the Moslem world, and religion and radio. Introduction of this last subject led in 1952 to the construction of new and expanded facilities in Stuart Hall for instruction in speech and radio under the imaginative direction of W. J. Beeners.

Earlier in 1940 cooperation between the Seminary and Princeton University had not been limited to the Seminary's obtaining its electricity from the University and providing heat to the University's Graduate College. At that time agreements had been developed whereby students in one institution could enroll for courses in the other in the fields of classical, Oriental and Old Testament languages.

Consistent with Mackay's concept of the ecumenical influence that Princeton Seminary should extend well beyond its student body and its own alumni, and well beyond the Presbyterian Church, was the re-establishment of a theological journal that would contain articles of significance for a wide audience concerned with fundamental religious issues. As a reincarnation of the defunct *Princeton Review*, the first issue of this new publication, *Theology Today*, appeared in 1944. As a result of one of Mackay's perambulatory musings the title page of the journal carried the words—"The Life of Man in the Light of God." Initially John A. Mackay was the editor, Hugh T. Kerr, Jr. the associate editor, and the Seminary provided a small subvention. In 1951 Kerr assumed the editorship of this religious quarterly which has been published continuously for nearly half a century under the general supervision of an ecumenical editorial board. As a consequence of the reputation that *Theology Today* soon established, its circulation by the mid-1950s exceeded 4,500, and by 1992 it had over 14,000 subscribers throughout the world.

At a later time the doctoral students at the Seminary initiated their own publication, entitled *Koinonia*, which enjoyed a much smaller distribution. From its inception this journal has endeavored to "promote interdisciplinary discussion and the exploration of new and emerging areas and issues in the study of religion," and has welcomed submission of articles by doctoral students at different institutions.

As part of its perceived broader educational mission Princeton Seminary cooperated during the latter part of the 1940s with various denominations located in the immediate geographical area to create the Princeton Leadership Training School. The Seminary provided the required physical facilities for the courses offered by the School on six successive Thursday evenings for church workers who in some years numbered as many as 350 from sixty-nine congregations involving eight denominations.

To accommodate these educational activities, to provide office

Theology 𝄯 Today

"our life in God's light"

Vol. XLIX, No. 1   April, 1992

THOMAS W. GILLESPIE, *Chair, Editorial Council*
HUGH T. KERR, *Senior Editor*
THOMAS G. LONG, *Editor*   PATRICK D. MILLER, JR., *Editor*
NANCY E. PIKE, *Business Manager*   MARSHA L. ROCHE, *Treasurer*

(Continued on the following page)

Theology Today
Title page of final issue edited by
Hugh T. Kerr

space for more faculty, and to house a larger student body, attention had to be given to the increasingly pressing physical needs of the Seminary. Although these needs had been recognized in earlier years, the necessary financing was not available during the decades that included World War I, the denominational near-schism of the 1920s, and the depression of the 1930s. But the needs remained and after the election of John Mackay to the presidency the Board of Trustees addressed its responsibility and resumed constructive planning to meet both the physical and financial needs of the Seminary.

Physical Expansion and Financial Needs

Following a number of years of deficit financing and no funds for construction of needed additional facilities, the Board of Trustees authorized soon after the inauguration of a new president that a fund raising campaign be undertaken. Henry S. Brown '00 was appointed vice president with specific responsibilities for financial development. A fund raising consulting firm was engaged, and the Forward Movement was launched with an announced eventual goal of $2.7 million, including $400,000 for a long anticipated campus center, and $52,450 for plant modernization.

It is not surprising that this endeavor did not meet with immediate success. Generally a long period of cultivation of prospective donors is required to be successful in raising large sums of money and for many years the Seminary had been distracted by other factors. The long depression was a deterrent and soon World War II created an obstacle in the path to financial solvency. Despite these difficulties the year 1940–41 ended with a small surplus, the first in five years, and other actions were undertaken to improve conditions.

In the year 1940–41 it was decided to institute for the first time in the history of the Seminary yearly tuition charges amounting to $50 for each student. Although small from the point of view of later years, the income produced from this source was at that time significantly helpful in a budget of less than $300,000. Furthermore, stimulated partially by the traveling choir under the supervision of the director of music, David Hugh Jones, gifts were being received. Influenced by the choir Mrs. George H. Whiteley of York, Pennsylvania, left a bequest of $50,000. Primarily through the efforts of Henry Brown the first of a series of gifts was received from Samuel Robinson whose total donations eventually exceeded a quarter of a million dollars. The widow of John H. Scheide, a deceased trustee, added to the scholarship fund with a gift of $43,000.

In 1941 the General Assembly gave attention to the financial conditions of its seminaries and designated a Seminary Sunday for church-wide collections for their benefit. By 1942 the Forward Movement had attained $250,000 and the budget was balanced for the third year in succession. Through the remainder of that decade the Seminary operated with a surplus in most years. To do so student charges were raised in increments so that by 1950 they amounted to $250. These raises were stimulated partially by the fact that tuition charges for military veterans were reimbursed by the federal government.

Between 1945 and 1955 the invested endowment increased from $3.9 to $5.1 million, a large part of which represented capital gains. Although the annual operating budgets had risen close to $1 million, the accumulated deficit was only $14,231. During this ten-year period the value of the plant had also been doubled to $2.6 million, largely by expansion of the campus and the construction of the Campus Center.

TENNENT CAMPUS

In 1943 the Hun School property, located only two blocks from the Seminary campus, became available for purchase at a price which was estimated to be about a fourth the cost of the original construction. The buildings, the first of which was constructed in 1924, contained facilities for classrooms, offices, student housing and feeding, and a gymnasium, in addition to several houses for faculty. By 1948 the Seminary spent $275,000 to acquire and improve this property where the School of Christian Education with its Charles G. Reigner Reading Room was located, where its women students were housed and fed, where athletics could be pursued in the gymnasium by all the students, and where needed accommodations were available for married students to supplement the rooms in Hodge Hall which had in recent years been assigned to married students with no children.

Since the former Tennent School of Christian Education with its assets were acquired by the Seminary, it was logical to name this new campus for William Tennent and the gymnasium for Mrs. Whiteley whose bequest was applied to the cost of this acquisition. The new gymnasium also made possible the conversion of the old refectory in 1945 into the administration building at a cost of $45,000, much of which was provided by alumni contributions. At the same time that this newer gymnasium was acquired, students had access to a bowling alley that the Seminary permitted the local Young Men's Christian Association to install that year in the basement of Stuart Hall.

MACKAY CAMPUS CENTER

Even with this campus expansion the long needed replacement for the defunct refectory continued to remain no farther along than the planning stages. After repeated appeals only $235,000 had been accumulated by 1947. This was forty-five years after the Board of Trustees, responding to appeals from the faculty, had appointed a Committee to Revive the Refectory which had been closed only several years earlier. In his reports to the trustees Stevenson had noted the need for common dining facilities, but for Mackay it was an absolute necessity that the Seminary should provide a campus center where a community spirit could be maintained among the faculty and a student body that was growing more diverse.

By 1951 over $416,000 had been accumulated for this project, less than half of the eventual cost, but sufficient to encourage the trustees to authorize the beginning of construction which was completed in time for the opening of the Seminary in September 1952. This was only the second new building, aside from the power plant, that had been constructed on the Seminary grounds since the completion of Hodge Hall in 1893. The Mackay Campus Center, as it was eventually named, provided space for a large dining room, kitchen, auditorium, faculty conference rooms, lounges, and later for the bookstore that had been started in 1938 largely by Leonard J. Trinterud '38 with a grant of $1,200 from the trustees. The final cost of construction was over $900,000 paid by 1,700 contributors, including $210,000 from five foundations.

The addition of this major facility tolled the death knell for the few remaining student eating clubs which then transferred their remaining assets to the Seminary, while many of their members nostalgically bemoaned their demise. The Campus Center did make an immediate change in the daily lives of the students. It also permitted the Seminary to extend its influence and make its facilities available to other groups. In the summer of 1954 the Synod of New Jersey met on the campus, followed by the Women's Synodical of New Jersey the next week. A few weeks later the Seminary was host to the World Presbyterian Alliance which was conducted in three official languages for some four hundred attendees representing sixty communions from forty countries. The Center also provided improved facilitates for the Institute of Theology, which that year had an enrollment of over three hundred, and the fifty-nine summer school students who were studying Greek or Hebrew. The presence of this building helped the Seminary as it strove to attain Mackay's goal of an ecumenically religious community.

SPEER LIBRARY

Although the trustees had created a committee in 1942 to study the issues related to the library needs, it was not until 1952 that the attention of the Board of Trustees, the administration and the faculty was concentrated directly on the library. Even with two buildings devoted exclusively to library purposes space was insufficient to house the growing collection of theologically related books, pamphlets, archival material and other historically important items. Consideration was given to enlarging Old Lenox, but this improvement was thought to be impractical. The building required too much repair and was not adaptable to the changing library demands which had increased rapidly with a larger student body and faculty, and more intensive study at both the undergraduate and graduate level.

Construction of a new building seemed assured when the General Assembly launched a $12 million drive to raise funds for its seminaries. Although the estimated cost of the building was $1.7 million, the Church-wide campaign allocated $1.35 million to Princeton leaving the balance to be raised directly by the Seminary, an amount that seemed attainable to the trustees. George T. Licht, who had designed the remodeling of Miller Chapel when it was moved and had drawn the plans for the Campus Center, was engaged as an architect to be assisted by his son and the firm of O'Connor and Kilham which had designed various buildings on the Princeton University campus. Endorsement had been granted earlier by the Board of Trustees to Mackay's proposal that the building be named for the deceased Robert E. Speer, the Board's recent chairman. Progress on this major undertaking seemed assured until objections were raised by many neighbors, including Albert Einstein. It was then and belatedly recognized that inadequate consideration had been given to the attitude of the community of Princeton.

When the public learned for the first time from an inadvertent and premature statement by the architect that Old Lenox would be razed, the reaction was immediate. Suddenly there was a clamor to preserve the old structure to which neighbors of the Seminary had developed an irreplaceable attachment. Pressure was applied to government officials to deny building permits. The local newspapers were filled with letters of condemnation of the Seminary, as well as rebuttals. Public meetings were held, one of which was convened by the Seminary in June 1955 at which Eugene Carson Blake '32, then a trustee and stated clerk of the General Assembly, presided, and Mackay read a carefully prepared statement to assuage the local objectors. Through negotiations and persuasion government authorization was finally attained, the objections subsided, both Lenox libraries were eventually razed, the cornerstone was laid in September 1956, and Speer Library was dedicated in October 1957. From this experience the Seminary learned that an educational institution must include its neighbors among the constituencies to be kept adequately informed of its actions and intentions.

During the 1940s and 1950s increasing attention was being given to its alumni, friends and potential friends, and the result was a gradual increase in most years of gifts and bequests. For example, in 1956 the Seminary was the recipient of a bequest of $422,000 for scholarship purposes from the daughter of John Dunlap Stokes, a member of the class of 1867, and in only six months of the year 1958 gifts amounting to $230,532 were received. As important as these contributions were, the election of two members of the Board of Trustees were over time to prove to be more significant for the financial interests of the Seminary.

In 1951 John M. Templeton, a financier known for his astute investment abilities and equally respected for his commitment to Christian ethics, joined the Board for which he served as chairman from 1967 to 1973 and 1979 to 1985. In 1955 Harry G. Kuch, another imaginative investment adviser, was elected to be a member of the Board. On the prudent advice of these two men the endowment of the Seminary, which was increased by 1959 to $9.6 million, was producing an income of over $300,000 a year. This was only the beginning of the financial legacy that Mackay's successors were to appreciate and enjoy.

But Mackay's immediate successor would also inherit the responsibility of constructing a new heating plant and of developing sufficient housing for the larger number of married students. An attempt to solve this latter issue was made in January 1959, a few months before Mackay's retirement, when ninety-one acres on the Great Road, a few miles north of Princeton, were purchased for $185,000 with the intention of constructing apartments on the property. Again neighbors raised objections which the trustees resolved on the advice of the new president by pursuing a different solution.

Administrative Developments

With the introduction of doctoral studies, with a larger enrollment, with an expanded campus, with increased financial operations it was inevitable that there would be a correlative need to increase the administrative structure of the Seminary. In retrospect it is somewhat surprising that a greater expansion did not develop earlier. The administrative staff, which was only marginally larger at the end of Mackay's twenty-two year tenure, in 1959 included only two new positions. In 1951 Orion C. Hopper '22 was appointed Alumni Secretary and Director of the Placement Bureau, and in 1955 J. Christy Wilson '19 was given the title of Dean of Field Service.

Even though there were few new positions during this period there were changes in personnel in the continuing positions. James K. Quay, the successor to Henry S. Brown, the first person to be appointed Vice President, was in turn succeeded by Joseph MacCarroll '35 who was given the title of Assistant to the President. Elmer G. Homrighausen '24 followed Edward H. Roberts as dean. On the other hand, George W. Loos, Jr. continued until 1964 as Treasurer and Business Manager, the position that he had held with different titles since 1928, and Kenneth S. Gapp '29 served as Assistant Librarian and then Librarian from 1934 to 1966. Retiring in the same year as Mackay, Edna Hatfield in 1959 completed forty-five years in a series of positions, first as secretary to Stevenson and finally as Registrar, a length of service that equalled Joseph Heatly Dulles, class of 1877, who was the Librarian from 1886 to 1931.

Changes also occurred between 1937 and 1959 in the composition of the Board of Trustees, not merely with respect to individuals but also on the basis of election. Prompted by the opportunity to encourage increased giving, Mackay suggested in 1943 that a board of lady managers or women's auxiliary be created. This was at a time when the Tennent School of Christian Education had been acquired from which eighty-two women would be graduated in the succeeding fifteen years. The tangible result of this proposal was the election in 1949 of Mrs. Charles O. (Mary Elizabeth White) Miller as the first of a succession of women to be members of the Board of Trustees. In that same year the General Assembly approved changes that permitted the Board to elect Presbyterian lay persons who need not be ruling elders. Concurrent with these developments the

Alumni Association petitioned the trustees for permission to nominate members for election to the Board. In 1947 this proposal was implemented with the selection of Frederick W. Evans '05 and C. Ralston Smith '37 as the first designated alumni trustees.

Greater attention was being accorded the alumni in various ways. The appointment of Orion C. Hopper '22 as both Alumni Secretary and Director of Placement Bureau provided tangible evidence of the desire of the Seminary to assist its alumni. The Alumni Conference, which had been reinstated in the fall of 1952, showed an increase in attendance of 170 within two years. Shortly after his appointment as vice president in 1948, Quay had designed and distributed to all alumni and friends calendars that would remind them not only of religious dates but also of the Seminary itself. In 1950 this publication was replaced by the *Spire*, a small magazine containing news of the Seminary, originally printed four times a year, then reduced to two and mailed to over 40,000 individuals, including 4,000 alumni. As an example of the increasing interest in alumni affairs and of the rapidly growing number of Presbyterians in Korea a Princeton Seminary Club for that country was organized on the suggestion of Syngman Rhee '11, then president of the Republic of Korea. The club first met in May 1954.

In 1955 the Alumni Office was able to report that during the previous nineteen years 881 undergraduates had become pastors, 162 assistant pastors or directors of Christian education, three college or seminary presidents, 104 professors and teachers, twenty-two executives of ecclesiastical bodies, seventy-four chaplains, 113 missionaries, and 103 in miscellaneous occupations, including non-religious activities. Possibly because alumni were encouraged to express more interest in their alma mater, members of the Association of Presbyterian University Pastors addressed a letter in 1956 to the president expressing their concerns with some developments at the Seminary that they claimed caused a loss of some faculty members and lack of interest in the Seminary on the part of potentially desirable students more liberally inclined. This letter stimulated a long conciliatory response from the president in which he emphasized the Seminary's considerable accomplishments, but it also reminded the administration and the trustees that the alumni and friends included diverse constituencies.

This exchange of correspondence coincided with the appointment of a trustees' committee on long-range planning that in 1957 recommended an enrollment of four hundred for the Master of Divinity degree, and a total of one hundred in the graduate programs. The committee further noted that additional and improved housing was a pressing necessity, and for these and other purposes additional funds were needed, a need that had been a constant factor ever since the Seminary was founded. The following year, after extensive inter-denominational discussions, the Presbyterian Church in the United States of America and the United Presbyterian Church of North America merged to form the United Presbyterian Church of the United States of America. Concurrently, the historical legal title of The Theological Seminary of the Presbyterian Church was largely disused and Princeton Theological Seminary became both its commonly used and official name.

Campus Life

One method of interpreting Mackay's definition of ecumenicity might be to compare the enrollment statistics for the Seminary between the early 1920s when as many as forty percent of the students were members of other denominations, with the years of his presidency when the number of Presbyterian master's degree students ranged between eighty and ninety percent. Albeit in many years among the non-Presbyterians there would be over forty denominations represented in the student body with candidates for doctoral degrees comprising a larger percentage of non-Presbyterians, such as Lutherans and Greek Orthodox. In any one year the enrollment would include students who had previously studied at as many as two hundred colleges and fifty seminaries in forty different states and twenty-five countries. Older men, and in time older women, were enrolling in the Seminary in preparation for second, even third careers.

This gradual expansion continued even after a special committee reported to the General Assembly in 1940 that there were too many seminaries for the number of students.

Although the total number of students tended to fluctuate, as it had in the past, the trend toward a larger enrollment continued from 1937 when it was 216 to 1959 when it reached 500. Following World War II as many as forty percent of the students were married, and the presence of women was further expanded after 1956 when the General Assembly followed the examples of the Congregationalists and Methodists who had much earlier in the century approved the ordination of women.

Fortunately, the acquisition of the Tennent Campus provided housing accommodations for women and some of the married students. Earlier, the designation of some rooms in Hodge Hall for married couples without children encouraged imaginative quips. Since the building was designed in the form of an angle, it soon became known colloquially as the "fertile crescent." But student imagination was not limited to campus witticisms.

With few exceptions students had enrolled in the seminary intent on preparing for some type of church ministry. They were interested in applying their learning and expending their energy in some evangelistic manner. This attitude was reinforced with the creation of the Department of Field Work in 1941 under the direction of J. Christy Wilson when most of the students were engaged part-time as pastors, assistant pastors, supply ministers, teachers of Christian education, or serving on deputations. Even before the establishment of a formal department there had been in 1939 four deputation teams comprising forty-eight members that visited eighty-four churches. During the next decade this evangelistic field work expanded in what then became known as Gospel Teams.

The purpose of this program was stated in the Seminary catalogue—"To provide our students with practical experience under the most favorable conditions; to bind the Seminary to a large number of congregations; to help the churches and the Presbyteries come to feel the Seminary helps them in their work—this is the immediate Seminary parish." In time a specified amount of field work by each undergraduate student was required for graduation. Over the years some imaginative programs were devised.

In 1949 William H. Cohea, Jr. and James R. Jackson, both members of the class of 1952, initiated a series of bull sessions with Princeton University students, a program that lead to inter-institutional deputations involving other colleges and universities. Later they were joined by Neill Q. Hamilton '51 and Bruce O. Larson '52, and the four spent the year 1952–53 visiting some thirty college campuses to stimulate student discussions of religious issues. At the same time Charles B. Templeton and John E. Turpin, both also of the class of 1952, organized during the spring vacation of their senior year in conjunction with the Somerville (New Jersey) Council of Churches a program in which seventy-eight seminary students made calls on residents of that community. And Warren W. Ost '51 directed a program of religious activities in the national parks for employees and visitors, an activity that he subsequently pursued as his vocational activity.

Some of these field activities conflicted with the religious services held on Sunday mornings in Miller Chapel where the attendance had decreased appreciably. After several years of hesitation the Board of Trustees approved their suspension in 1940, and four years later the weekly academic schedule was further altered when evening and Saturday morning classes were discontinued. The end to the Sunday service did not mean a lessening of religious interest. Partially to compensate, a Theological Society was organized to provide for discussion sessions. In each semester a day was devoted to religious and inspirational lectures. With encouragement from the Student Council small groups of students and faculty held series of retreats over weekends throughout each year. And in 1958 small group sessions were organized for the purpose of relieving emotional tensions that inevitably occur with a small percentage of any student body.

Some of the field activities in which the students were involved provided no financial remuneration. On the other hand,

David Hugh Jones
a member of the faculty from 1939 to 1970
conducting the student choir

most did provide a stipend, a godsend since the tuition was increasing almost yearly. In 1940 the tuition was $50 and the
total basic yearly charges amounted to $440; by 1958 tuition
had been increased ten-fold and the estimated total basic cost
was $1,325. Scholarships were significantly helpful but not as
plentiful as they became in later years.

The student activity that provided students with credit for
field work and indirectly provided a stimulus for financial donations to the Seminary was the traveling choir, and over the
years travel it did. Under the direction of David Hugh Jones
from 1942 to 1970 the choir sang in churches and assembly
halls in every state and many foreign countries: Canada, Cuba,
Guatemala, Japan, Korea, Mexico. It sang for recordings and
presented concerts for radio audiences, always "to proclaim the
Christian Gospel through Scripture, song and testimony."

A vivid description of the choir's experiences was reported by Peter R. McKenzie '50 in the winter 1949 issue of the *Princeton Seminary Bulletin.*

Ten thousand miles is a long way to go—especially if you sing every day and three times on Sunday . . . [The choir has three purposes]— To present the Gospel through the great music of the Church, to tell why they were entering the ministry, and to place before congregations the pressing need for more ministers, and their responsibilities in meeting it.

During the fifty days of traveling, the choir sang in churches, colleges, missions and a prison; they appeared in public halls and in private homes, in hospitals and schools, in camps and on picnics. They slept in farmhouses and in mansions, ate strawberry-shortcake and pudding, and sang in fresh white shirts and dusty, grey ones, rode in five automobiles and pushed them through deep mudholes.

By 1958 there were, in addition to the traveling choir, four other singing groups including a recently organized women's choir. Then after 1970 interest flagged, when, following Jones' retirement in that year, the faculty discontinued granting field work credit for participation in the choir.

Words of Fulfillment

In anticipation of his retirement three years hence Mackay had observed at the April 1956 meeting of the Board of Trustees that

in these last years, something new has been added to our Princeton tradition, a new sense of the Church Universal which the followers of John Calvin had tended to lose. Throughout the Protestant world, and to a special degree on this campus, a new sense of the reality of the Church has been born, and a new commitment made to the Church Universal . . .

The direction in which we should move would seem to be this. Let Princeton Seminary continue to be what it has always been, a rallying point for evangelical loyalty in many churches. Let it also be a center where the very best in one great tradition, namely the Reformed, shall be expressed in a dynamic way, and where facilities shall be provided to promote the development of those who are interested in both piety and learning.

Throughout the world and over a period of four decades Mackay had preached his ecumenical theology based on conservative Scottish convictions. His appointed and elected positions of responsibility were numerous: chairman of the International Missionary Council, president of the American Association of Theological Schools, first chairman of the Council on Theological Education of the Presbyterian Church, and active in many world and national inter-denominational organizations. When he exercised his greatest influence he was Moderator of the General Assembly of the Presbyterian Church in the U.S.A. whose membership was then approaching three million in a total of sixty million Protestants in the United States. In the position of Moderator he issued a widely published and quoted "Letter to Presbyterians" on September 2, 1953 that gently and penetratingly castigated in moral and social terms the excesses of unproven political defamation in which members of the United States Congress were then engaged.

His final year was blighted only by a lawsuit initiated by an assistant professor whose appointment was terminated and who based his claims on the Seminary's failure to follow accepted academic procedures in promotion. This incident led to the subsequent placing of the Seminary on the list of censured institutions by the American Association of University Professors. At the same time, it led during the early part of the next administration to the appropriate and needed codification of bylaws that limited the number of years in which an individual was permitted to serve on the faculty without tenure. Undeterred but saddened by this episode Mackay in his final report to the trustees in April 1959 spoke of the battles that had been "won without the creation of bitterness or division in the Church or Seminary constituency."

In these successes he included the increasing financial support provided to theological education from the general mission budget of the Presbyterian Church, the establishment of the publication *Theology Today,* and the development of graduate studies in theology. To these he added—"It is the struggle to create ecumenical reality across the frontiers of denominational diversity, and to achieve this under the auspices of a classical Christian tradition which cannot be true to itself without putting the Church Universal above sectarian glory." In these and other pronouncements Mackay prepared the path for his successor.

7

Song of Songs

SOLOMON

When the Board of Trustees announced in October 1958 the name of the successor to John Mackay as president of Princeton Theological Seminary there were many who responded with the query, "Who is James I. McCord?" The thirty-nine year old theologian from Texas was not yet well known even though he had already demonstrated qualities that soon made him a world-wide leader of Reformed Christianity, the same qualities that he exerted in the further revitalization of Princeton Seminary during his twenty-four year incumbency.

McCord, born in 1919 in Rusk, Texas, was a graduate of Austin College, Austin Theological Seminary, and of the University of Texas where he both taught and obtained a master's degree. Before he returned to Austin Seminary in 1944 as Professor of Systematic Theology and then Dean he had pursued studies at Harvard University and held pastorates in Manchester, New Hampshire, and in Austin. As an indefatigable student and an insatiable reader he later studied at New College in Edinburgh, Scotland. With his prodigious memory, sound judgment, and resonant voice he was impressive in speaking whether in conversation with an individual in an office, or to a committee in a conference room, or to an assembly in a church.

Eugene Carson Blake '32, then stated clerk of the General Assembly and chairman of the trustees' selection committee, was acquainted with McCord who had been chairman of the Committee on World Missions of the Presbyterian Church of the United States as well as a member of several of its Assembly's interim committees. McCord was also becoming known for his imaginative leadership in various educational and theological organizations, including the World Alliance of Reformed

Churches, the World Council of Churches, the American Association of Theological Schools, and the Advanced Religious Study Foundation. After meeting with Dean McCord the selection committee, consisting of Arthur M. Adams '34, E. Harris Harbison, W. Sherman Skinner, '30, John M. Templeton, and Blake, unanimously proposed his election to the presidency of the Seminary, a recommendation that was heartily endorsed by the Board of Trustees.

Assuming his new duties in the late summer of 1959 McCord's presence and manner of operation were immediately felt by everyone closely associated with the Seminary. He started on the run and never stopped running until several years after he had retired in 1983 to become chancellor of the Center of Theological Inquiry, a new enterprise that had been his long-standing dream. One of his admiring colleagues observed that he was like a wheel-horse or a rechargeable battery, always active, thinking, planning, organizing. As the years progressed his momentum propelled him into so many world-wide theological activities that he seemed no sooner to have returned to the campus than he had departed for another religious commitment.

Extending Mackay's dream of ecumenicity, McCord, while loyal to the Presbyterian Church, envisioned an interfaith dialogue that included not only other Protestant denominations but also Roman and Orthodox Catholics. These concepts were represented in appointments to the Seminary faculty and in formal cooperation with the Roman Catholic Diocese of Trenton. The new president was a brilliant organizer and facilitator with an ability to implement ideas whether they were his or those which he endorsed. He was a driving force both in the Seminary and the Presbyterian Church, and at the same time served in a pastoral relationship with the members of the faculty and staff, as well as many of the students.

His twenty-four year presidency represented a dynamic period of growth and development in the history of the Seminary. Despite initial years of economic uncertainty both the size of the faculty and the student body were expanded; the curriculum and degree programs were increased; the campus facilities and the library collections were enlarged; and the financial resources of the institution were multiplied many times.

McCord believed that the primary purpose of the Seminary was to educate and train the professional leadership of the Church and that its faculty should assist the Church in the development of its program by extending the body of theological knowledge. With this guiding principle he established and pursued his priorities of strengthening Princeton Seminary.

He initiated a program of physical renovation of the campus so that the continuation of deferred maintenance would not later place an unsupportable burden on the institution and compete with the growing financial demands for the academic programs of the future. At the same time, he extended the Seminary's financial efforts and sought an endowment for all of the established professorships as well as for the many other needs of a vibrant theological seminary.

Undergirding these activities was a recognition that the enormous expansion in knowledge of the twentieth century would place even further pressures on Christian theology to analyze its own roots and its relationship to other disciplines. In a personal note to the author of this narrative history Professor James F. Armstrong observed that McCord repeatedly addressed the importance of "creative, interdisciplinary research to theology so that it would be better prepared to cooperate in the construction of new paradigms for religion and society." His conceptions influenced the appointment of members of the faculty and his perseverance led to the creation of the Center of Theological Inquiry. Furthermore, the added momentum that was generated during the McCord administration did not wane on his retirement.

His successor, Thomas W. Gillespie, shortly after his accession to the presidency in 1983 reiterated the purpose of the seminary and noted "that the state of theology today, at least in the United States, has been determined more by the departments of graduate schools of religion than by theological seminaries." In this same article he observed that "the Church has allowed theology to become the private preserve of the experts. The laity defer to the ordained ministry, while our ministers

James I. McCord
President of the Seminary from 1959 to 1983
conversing with Professor J. Christiaan Beker

defer to the professional theologians. If theology is basically the *wisdom* of faith, then it belongs to the entire community of faith. . . ." (*PTS Alumni News*, No. 4, 1984) Based on this conviction Gillespie proceeded to pursue the goal of reclaiming and reinterpreting the Reformed faith in a Presbyterian Church in need of reinvigoration at the same time that cordial and ecumenical relationships were maintained with many different theological denominations.

Thomas Gillespie, a native Californian, was born in 1928. After service in the United States Marine Corps and completion of his undergraduate studies at George Pepperdine College, he was graduated from Princeton Seminary in 1954 at which time he was awarded the Archibald Alexander Hodge Prize in Sys-

Thomas W. Gillespie
President of the Seminary since 1983
conversing with a friend

tematic Theology. Following his ordination and concurrent
with his serving as the pastor of Presbyterian churches in Gar-
den Grove and Burlingame, California, he completed further
studies and obtained the degree of doctor of philosophy from
Claremont Graduate School.

In returning to the Seminary of which he was an alumnus
Gillespie needed few introductions and was easily able to establish his innate collegial mode of administration. The institution
continued, however, to maintain the momentum that had prevailed during the years of McCord's incumbency. In contrast to
the nineteenth century when the life and theology of the Seminary seemed in the view of many later historians to be less
responsive to the dynamic events occurring in society, during

the latter third of the twentieth century Princeton Seminary was aware of and reacted to the economic and political, the military and pacifist, and the moral issues that have made this period one of the more dynamic eras of recorded history.

Societal Dynamics

Life has been, is, and always will be filled with uncertainties. The unpredictable future is one of the factors that inspires men and women to depend upon religion for their salvation. As much as some theologians might deny that economic, political, or social factors affect religions there has been a super-abundance of evidence throughout history that these forces, as well as cataclysmic events, have stimulated religious reverence for an Unseen Being that directs the destiny of the world. Furthermore, wars of religion, denominational schisms, theological conflicts have affected all faiths. The Presbyterians have not been the only denomination or religious body to undergo periods of theological conflict and schism.

No such convulsions affected the Presbyterians, however, in the latter part of the twentieth century when the Church was strengthened by the reunion in 1983 of the two branches that had separated from each other at the time of the Civil War more than a century earlier. The resulting Presbyterian Church in the U.S.A., a united but smaller denomination in membership than a few years earlier, continued to support a school of Christian education and ten seminaries of which Princeton Theological Seminary was and has continued to be the largest. This Seminary's dynamic development during the recent thirty-three years of its history has occurred in an era that has been punctuated with events which become clouded in one's memory because of their multiplicity but which cumulatively have influenced the trustees, the faculty, the students, and the alumnae/alumni as they have exerted their collective influence in fashioning the direction that Princeton Seminary has pursued.

The development of the Seminary during McCord's administration and since the arrival of his successor can be better understood when one reflects on just a few of the many diverse events that have occurred in society during their era that so far has extended over a third of a century. The technological developments of computers and telecommunications have affected all segments of society, including seminaries. Civil rights, the ordination of women, the practice of abortion, and the growth of the AIDS epidemic are just a few of the issues with which theological professors and seminary students have been confronted in this period. And the economic recession of the early 1990s following the excesses of the 1980s created not only ethical dilemmas for some theologians but affected the planning and operations of all denominations, their individual congregations, and their seminaries. In being influenced by these forces Princeton Seminary has been no exception. All of society was being affected, not the least our many religious denominations.

Twenty years earlier public opinion polls were indicating a widespread conception that the influence of religion was declining, just as membership in the Presbyterian Church was receding, and various religious observers were employing the phrase, "the death of God."

In 1981 the author of a cultural history of religion in America wrote:

The obvious shortcoming here is that theology is increasingly unnecessary to the life of religious institutions. Doctrinal beliefs become matters of opinion which figure less prominently in an individual's choice of churches or church programs. Social class, liturgical style, and moral tone replace doctrine as ways of characterizing churches. . . . Many areas of social life have been liberated from religious control. Education, law, the state, and the economy have been secularized, and the church does not orient the modern city as it did the town square. (Moseley, p. 63 & p. 145)

Despite these and other observations of religious gloom Princeton Theological Seminary continued to thrive and to be a constructive theological force during the McCord and Gillespie eras as it maintained its commitment to Presbyterian traditions. Other than this observation this concluding chapter will, in view of the recency of this era, be more factual than interpretive. A more adequate analysis and interpretation will be the responsibility of future historians of religion.

Financial Growth

Although neither financial resources nor physical facilities are the most important features of a theological seminary, they do present a measurable description of an institution. When McCord arrived in Princeton in 1959 he was immediately confronted with a financial statement that indicated the Seminary was operating on a deficit budget. By the end of his first year, with a budget of less than $2 million, the accumulated deficits amounted to $800,000, large but less than the deficit that would be incurred in a single year nearly two decades later. To help stem the losses, tuition charges were raised to $500 for each student whose total basic yearly costs with room and board amounted to $1,200.

During the following three decades a delicate balancing act was pursued to avoid too many years of successive deficits and at the same time to meet the competing demands of inflation, the need for salary increases and plant maintenance, and the financial burdens that most students faced. The progressive financial accomplishments of the Seminary attest to the acumen, imagination, and prudent management of the trustees and administration, and also to the generosity and support of the innumerable and diverse friends that the Seminary had developed over many years.

These years were marked by almost consistent annual increases in nearly every aspect of the budget. By 1992 the total yearly operating budget was over $24 million following a year that was completed with an unusual surplus of half a million dollars. The endowment, which by then was producing over sixty percent of the income for the Seminary compared with less than twenty percent thirty years earlier, had reached a market value of over $400 million as the result of many generous gifts and bequests and the astute investment strategy of John Templeton.

Among the various recommendations, which Templeton proposed and the Board of Trustees endorsed, one involved the re-investment each year of a small percentage of the income from endowment in order to provide for future needs. Also, all endowment funds were invested in pooled accounts which provided greater flexibility and financial benefits to each of the funds. These pooled accounts did not include over seven million dollars held by other organizations the income of which was designated for Seminary purposes.

In October 1986, recognizing that the investment of funds of such magnitude entailed moral responsibilities, the Board of Trustees adopted a statement of principle from which the following declaration has been extracted.

In fulfilling its fiduciary responsibilities, the Board of Trustees seeks to invest available funds in ways which are consistent with its understanding of the Christian gospel. It shares the vision of the Reformed theological tradition that the world, including the world of business, is the arena for the glorification of God. Investments are thus by definition matters of Christian stewardship which are subject to ethical consideration informed by Christian faith.

In contrast to other seminaries in which student tuition and fees provided over fifty percent of the income, such fees at Princeton in 1992 were comprising less than twenty percent of the budget. Nevertheless, the basic expenses of tuition, room, board and books amounted to $11,000 for each master's degree student, eighty-eight percent of whom were receiving some financial assistance. Even with relatively generous student aid and income from part-time employment, as many as a third of the graduates receiving the master's degree left the Seminary with sizable debts, much of which had been incurred during their undergraduate college years.

During this period there was a steady and marked decrease not only in the percentage but also in the amount of receipts from the General Assembly. Fortunately, gifts from other sources more than compensated for this reduction and constituted a major factor in the financial growth of Princeton Seminary. These donations included annuities, which provided generous return to the donors during their lives, bequests and direct donations from foundations, churches, corporations, and individuals who designated their gifts either for endowment, general operating costs and specific programs, or addition to or rehabilitation of existing physical facilities.

Despite the fact that the Seminary was not eligible for government grants because of its religious function, that it understandably had few wealthy alumni, and that most corporations and many foundations were hesitant to support theological education, Princeton Seminary was especially successful in raising funds to meet its continuing and expanding needs. From its earliest days parishes, presbyteries, synods and individuals provided financial assistance for students, especially in the form of scholarships. Over the years, commencing in the latter part of the nineteenth century, lectureships and professorships were established as memorials to alumni, professors, and other friends of the Seminary, and by 1992 most of these had been fully funded. Between 1976 and 1986 the Seminary raised in a sesquicentennial campaign over $36 million, and then in a subsequent campaign that ended in December 1990 another $22 million was obtained for such purposes as new construction, plant rehabilitation, faculty salaries, and the Asian-American program.

In contrast to the nineteenth century when a few major donors could readily be identified among the large number who made smaller donations, there were so many contributors of large sums of money in the latter part of the twentieth century that it is appropriate to identify only one. She was Mrs. Charles T. Newcomb, a long-time friend of Arthur M. Adams '34, who had been a trustee before he assumed the position of dean of the Seminary. He encouraged Charlotte Newcomb's interest that led to the bequest of one-half of her estate to the Seminary. In 1979–80 Princeton was the recipient of $16.3 million, the largest gift it had ever received. Of these funds $6 million were assigned to endowment for continuing education, field education, the library and professorships. The remainder covered the expenses entailed in renovating several of the nineteenth century campus buildings and the costs related to the purchase and rehabilitation of a previously acquired married students' housing complex that was renamed the Charlotte Rachel Wilson Apartments, in memory of Mrs. Newcomb's mother.

With such financial success one might assume, in the words of the twenty-third psalm, that the Seminary's "cup runneth over." It is true that Princeton Seminary was anointed with economic resources, but the financial needs continued unabated as inflation persisted to affect the economy, even at a slower pace, and as the Seminary aspired to strengthen its resources in anticipation of the unknown demands of the twenty-first century.

Physical Expansion

Following World War II the composition of the student body included a growing number of married students for only a small percentage of whom the Seminary was capable of providing housing accommodations. This was an issue which Mackay had repeatedly called to the attention of the trustees. Shortly before his retirement property had been acquired along the Great Road, a few miles north of the campus. Opposition from potential neighbors for the construction of married student housing on this location was sufficiently intense, and the zoning problems were sufficiently complex that soon after McCord's arrival the property was sold.

The issue of married student housing remained unresolved until 1965. On June tenth of that year a notice of sheriff's sale of a completed two-year old housing complex with two hundred apartments was announced. After feverish analyses and consultations the Seminary submitted a bid on June seventeenth and shortly thereafter acquired title to the property which included twenty-five buildings on fifty-two acres which were soon increased to seventy-eight acres along a main highway several miles south of the campus and contiguous to a public recreation area. Thus continued an era of physical growth and attention to the needs for rehabilitation of all the Seminary's physical facilities.

Earlier in 1962 with the initiation of offerings in continuing education it was necessary to provide adequate accommodations

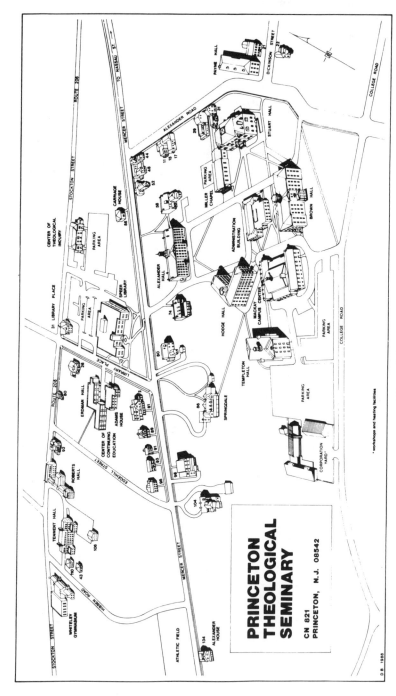

Map of the Campus

Subsequent to its initial drawing in 1988, 31 Library Place was renamed Lenox House for the visiting ministers who enrolled in this program, one of the first of its kind offered by any seminary in the United States. The house at 12 Library Place across the street from Speer Library became available, and with the assistance of a grant from the James Foundation it was purchased for $125,000, renovated, and some years later named Adams house in honor of Dean Arthur M. Adams.

During the middle of the 1960s the acquisition of property continued to be an absorbing issue for the trustees and administration. In a complicated three-way negotiation with the Borough of Princeton and Miss Fine's School, which was being merged with Princeton Country Day School at a new location, the Seminary acquired for $300,000 the land contiguous to Speer Library on which the historic Thomson House stood that had served as the Borough Hall. Included in the purchase was the building then and since known as the Carriage House which was soon converted for use for seminars and faculty offices. In customary Princeton manner there was much public objection to the razing of Thomson House, which had been designed by Charles Steadman and built in 1826 by Richard Stockton, known as the "Duke," for his daughter Josephine Stockton. She was married to John R. Thomson, a United States Senator, for whom the building was later named. By the time of its acquisition the structure had deteriorated past the stage of economic usefulness and was subject to possible condemnation. Thus, the site was available in the 1980s as the location for the Center of Theological Inquiry.

Concurrent with these developments sixty-six acres located several miles north of Princeton on Mount Lucas Road were acquired in 1964 after the plan for married student housing on the Great Road had been aborted and just before the Charlotte Rachel Wilson Apartments became available. William E. Lawder, who had that year begun his service of twenty-two years as business manager and treasurer, was acquainted with a quiet, unassuming bachelor, and generous Presbyterian. William Habada had been born in Czechoslovakia, raised in an orphanage in the United States, lived in a frugal manner relying upon none of the modern conveniences, and purchased property with his modest savings. As a result of Lawder's association with Ha-bada this land was acquired on the basis of a deferred annuity trust which on the latter's death provided a substantial bequest to be added to the Seminary's endowment. Two decades later this area, whose principal street was named for the second president, J. Ross Stevenson, was developed to provide housing for members of the enlarged faculty which could no longer be accommodated in the two and one-half dozen houses adjacent to and owned by the Seminary.

These physical acquisitions were complemented by the construction of additional facilities on the campus. In 1965 the boiler failed in the heating plant that had been in continuous operation since 1908. Fortunately, plans had already been initiated for the plant's replacement which now became imperative. The power lines were attached to those of Princeton University which provided service temporarily until the new Corporation Yard with its modern heating plant and maintenance facilities was completed in 1967. Designed by Michael P. Erdman, the grandson of Professor Charles E. Erdman, this structure was accorded much favorable recognition for its aesthetic and utilitarian design.

In 1969–70 construction of a dormitory with accommodations for eighty men and women students, a visiting lecturer suite, and seminar room was completed next to the Center of Continuing Education. Named for Professor Erdman the building was built on property previously owned and occupied by the Erdmans and was also designed by his grandson.

Throughout these three decades campus maintenance and improvements continued at a steady pace. Miller Chapel was air conditioned, renovated and a new fifty-two stop Moller organ installed. Hodge Hall was remodeled with faculty offices installed on the first floor. Alexander, Brown and Stuart Halls were completely rehabilitated as were the buildings on the Tennent campus. Here the three wings of Roberts Hall, named for Edward H. Roberts '23 who had served on the faculty and in various administrative positions from 1930 until his death in 1954, were dedicated to three women: Mrs. Margaret Weyerhaeuser Harmon, a former trustee, Mrs. Mary S. Miller, a generous friend, and Mrs. Georgette S. Raguso, a graduate of the former Tennent College of Christian Education.

Facilities were further improved with the remodeling and later enlargement of the Administration Building and Adams House, the installation and expansion of air conditioning equipment for the campus, and the construction of the Charlotte Newcomb Center with its study and recreation accommodations. Later an indoor swimming pool was constructed for the benefit of the residents in the Charlotte Rachel Wilson Apartments. The streets in this housing complex had previously been named for two former officers of the Board of Trustees, Peter K. Emmons '15 and Benjamin K. Farber '09, and two former highly respected professors, Frederick W. Loetscher '00 and Donald Wheeler.

The 1980s ended with the construction of a magnificent building designed not merely to provide additional space for administrative offices but to accommodate a modern computer center and an especially well-equipped speech and media center. Financed by many generous contributions, the building was completed in 1989 and named for John and Irene Templeton in recognition of the trustee who had been primarily responsible for the financial stability and strength of the Seminary.

By 1991, with the exception of the Campus Center, all major buildings had been completely renovated within a period of twelve years. During the summers of 1991 and 1992 this building, which had in 1984 been named in honor of John A. Mackay, was rehabilitated and brought to the standards of the other structures on the campus.

Also in 1992 construction began on a multi-million dollar major expansion of Speer Library. When completed this addition will be named the Henry Luce III Library and will include a major section dedicated to William H. Scheide, each of whom has been a long-time, generous trustee of the Seminary.

With all of these physical developments the trustees and administration continuously demonstrated and continued to demonstrate their awareness that responsible management will find the means to provide good facilities and avoid deferred maintenance which has always proven to be more costly in the long run.

Seminary Governance

During the latter part of the twentieth century the administrations of most educational institutions expanded in response to the increasing expectations of more diverse student bodies, the inclusion of educational programs for both degree candidates and other professional and lay persons, the introduction of computer and telecommunication technologies, the growing pressures to solicit funds in larger and larger amounts, and the expanding regulations of federal, state and local governments. Princeton Theological Seminary was forced to respond to all of these developments to which the growth in its administrative staff bears witness.

Shortly after the arrival of McCord it became obvious that the administrative staff was insufficient to fulfill the demands that were developing. Student services had to be increased, directors of expanding educational programs had to be appointed, personnel had to be added to direct the growing emphasis on external relations and fund raising, and supporting staff had to be employed for these operations and the maintenance of the enlarged campus with its added facilities. By 1992 the administrative and clerical-secretarial staff was more than three times as large as thirty years earlier, the staff of the library nearly twice as large, the maintenance personnel fifty percent larger, whereas appointments to the full-time faculty, exclusive of visiting professors and lecturers, grew at a smaller rate.

With this expansion in personnel, which was begun in 1959, there were through the succeeding decades changes in the structure of the faculty with more explicit definitions and assigned responsibilities, reorganizations from time to time of the administrative staff, and revisions in operating procedures in the administrative offices as a result, to a large extent, of the introduction of computers. These changes did not, however, affect the loyalty to the Seminary that its personnel exhibited from the earliest days of Archibald Alexander. Longevity of service, a characteristic of its employees, was epitomized by Clarence E. Reed who retired as director of housing in 1981 after forty-seven years of service to the Seminary.

Membership on the Board of Trustees has also been characterized by a devotion to the institution and its basic purpose of educating and training men and women for religious service to society. Continuity has been maintained by the faithfulness of many trustees who have accepted re-election to the Board, the size and composition of which was altered on several occasions by amendments to the charter and by-laws. In 1962 the commonly used name of Princeton Theological Seminary was legally approved as an alternative for the original title and at the same time the Presbyterian lay members of the Board were no longer required to be ruling elders.

Following the reunion in 1983 of the two Presbyterian bodies that had been separated since the time of the Civil War, the General Assembly adopted further liberalizing policies relating to its seminaries. Assembly action was now limited only to what in essence was endorsement of the election of trustees and the president. By Seminary policy the latter was required to be a member of the Presbyterian Church. The Board of Trustees of the Seminary was granted final authority in the appointment of professors who were expected to be committed to the Christian faith but need not be members of the Presbyterian denomination. The size of the Board had been increased to forty with no more than eighteen to be ordained ministers and no more than twenty-two lay communicants of the Presbyterian Church. Retirement of trustees at age seventy-five was mandated so that by 1992 David Brainerd Watermulder '45 was the only active member of the Board who had served during the administrations of Mackay, McCord and Gillespie. Years earlier women and members of ethnic and racial minorities had been elected to membership on the Board.

Aware of the need for more time to consider in a deliberative manner the rapid social changes that were impinging on the Seminary the trustees held retreats of several days in the fall at locations away from Princeton, and on occasions jointly with the faculty. In January 1974 the first mid-winter meeting of the

Board to be held away from the campus was made possible primarily through the generosity of a member of the board, who later provided an endowment to establish such meetings on a regular basis. The location of the first such meeting was Florida where another trustee, Clem E. Bininger '34, pastor of the First Presbyterian Church in Fort Lauderdale, provided facilities that were conducive to collective reflection and planning. It was apparent that careful reflection was necessary as the dynamic forces of society were affecting all seminaries.

Inflation was increasing the costs of operating Princeton Seminary and causing a growing need for financial assistance on the part of students. At the same time total membership in the main-line denominations was declining. The Presbyterians suffered such losses that placement of seminary graduates became an issue of frequent concern, and financial support for Princeton Seminary from the General Assembly began a major decline.

Public debates were raised over the place of the church in society, the role and image of the ministry, and the historically divisive conflict between tradition versus experience and feeling in religion, or in the words of the 1811 Plan for the Seminary, between vital piety and sound theological learning. Attitudes toward ecumenism and missions were changing. Furthermore, the growth of pluralism both in society and on the campus required more attention to the concerns of women, blacks, Hispanics, Korean-American, and other groups which were now represented in the student body in larger numbers.

As all of these events were unfolding the trustees were making decisions that affected all aspects of Princeton Seminary, especially appointments to the faculty and approval of academic programs. The recognition by the trustees of their responsibilities is best expressed in a statement contained in the minutes of the Board of Trustees at its October 1984 meeting.

There is a constant tension among the substantial aims of the Seminary to train dedicated, skilled, learned, cultivated ministers for congregations and the other objectives, namely, to train scholars in the PhD level to teach in seminaries, colleges, etc.; to develop and provide key leadership for the church at large, to offer continuing education for ministers, and to provide biblical and ethical instruction for laymen on a sophisticated level for scientists, professional business people, and executive managers.

On top of these categories competing for resources is another tension whether the Seminary should work primarily for the Presbyterian family or for the ecumenical church sphere, or for both.

It was concluded that it was best for the time being "to hold these several spheres of tension in a healthy dynamic balance." As with all of society such tensions continued and they may be expected to continue indefinitely and long into the future.

Faculty Appointments

Among the first issues that McCord had to face on his arrival in Princeton was the law suit over academic appointments and the official censure of the Seminary by the American Association of University Professors. In his direct and effective manner he recognized the problems involved and determined to resolve them constructively as rapidly as possible. This he was able to accomplish and so could then turn with fewer distractions to the selection of new members for the faculty, which, as on previous occasions, was in need of "new blood."

Faculty appointments had been intentionally deferred during the final several years of Mackay's presidency awaiting the completion of a long-range planning study and the arrival of his successor. As a consequence, within only the first five years of his assuming the presidency McCord was involved in the appointment of twenty-five men and women to the faculty, including both professors and instructors. (Unfortunately, because of their number, the nature of this narrative history does not provide space for their individual identification by name.) With the establishment of additional professorships and the adoption of the policy limiting the length of appointments for younger members without tenure, the personnel of the faculty underwent more rapid changes than had prevailed previously with the exception of the early years in the 1930s. Furthermore, the availability of retirement benefits eliminated the ne-

James I. McCord and Faculty Colleagues, 1982

First row (left to right): D. L. Migliore, J. E. Loder, D. T. Jenkins,
D. Allen, J. N. Lapsley, Jr., President McCord, K. E. McVey,
L. G. Livezey, P. W. Meyer, A. D. Duba; *second row:*
B. W. Anderson, J. F. Armstrong, S. H. Lee, B. M. Metzger,
J. R. Nichols, S. R. Brown, G. W. Hanson, R. S. Armstrong,
E. G. Edwards, J. H. Nichols; *third row:* D. E. Capps,
K. Froelich, F. A. Gardner, C. C. West, C. A. Ryerson III,
S. H. Moffett, B. C. Ollenburger, D. R. Adams, J. C. Beker;
fourth row: J. T. Butler, G. Winter, H. T. Kerr, Jr.,
W. Brower, D. Macleod, G. R. Jacks, K. D. Sakenfeld; *fifth row:*
C. H. Massa, D. C. Wyckoff, E. H. Dowey, Jr.

cessity of members of the faculty endeavoring to remain active into their seventies as many did in the nineteenth century.

As a result of the larger than usual number of faculty positions to be filled it was possible to respond more readily to changes in social attitudes and include able women and members of minority groups. While members of the faculty continued to be primarily white male Presbyterians, in time the proportion of women markedly increased, as well as the numbers from other races and denominations, and with the expansion of the teaching staff the ratio of faculty to students was slightly lowered.

By 1991–1992 the faculty, excluding lecturers, had been increased to forty-eight, two-thirds of whom were Presbyterians. The others represented eleven different Christian denominations, including one Roman Catholic and two who were not affiliated with traditional denominations. With few exceptions all had academic doctoral degrees; their average age was fifty-two, and by 1992 the majority had served on the faculty less than ten years. In contrast to the nineteenth century and the early years of the twentieth century Princeton Seminary had ceased to be an inbred institution.

Academic Programs

With the changes in faculty personnel and with the dynamic changes that affected all aspects of society, including the ministry, it was inevitable and predictable that in the McCord and Gillespie eras there would be additions to and revisions in the academic programs offered at Princeton Theological Seminary. In reviewing the educational developments of the Seminary during its one hundred and eighty year history, one may be justified in observing that there seemed to be more curricular additions and revisions in the period subsequent to 1959 than in all the previous years since 1812.

In contrast to the usual academic practice of instituting curricular modifications with glacial rapidity, the curricular changes in the 1960s and 1970s at the Seminary appear to have been like a river in a narrow tree-lined basin that suddenly flows into wide open, rapidly descending terrain. Not only were curricular options markedly enlarged but academic vitality was evident in various directions.

In 1961 major revisions were instituted in the Bachelor of Divinity program. As stated in the faculty announcement, those changes were instituted "to permit the maximum of flexibility and independence consonant with a broad theological foundation." It was further declared that "general examinations should constitute the primary focus of the student's course and independent reading." With an intent to avoid large lecture and survey courses each bachelor's degree candidate was required to complete seventy-eight credit hours within the three-year program including courses in Greek and Hebrew. To conform with Princeton University the calendar was revised on the basis of two semesters a year in place of the three-quarter system, and the following year all bachelor of divinity candidates were required to participate in some form of field education.

The junior, or first year, was devoted to pursuance of basic courses in each of the four departments; the middlers had a broader program, and the seniors pursued a major field of study. In September 1982 as part of a long-range planning report Charles C. West, then Academic Dean of the Seminary, outlined for the trustees the designated responsibilities of the four academic departments.

The *Biblical Department* is responsible, within each of the Testaments, for providing a diversified study of Scripture against its historical background, a theological understanding of the biblical message, and some foundations for the communication of biblical understanding in the modern world.

The *History Department* is commissioned with the broad task of interpreting the life and tradition of the Christian Church as it interacts with the social, philosophical, cultural, and scientific history of the past 2,000 years.

The *Theology Department* has as its major responsibility the interpretation of the biblical sources and the historical experience of the church's faith in terms that are coherent and meaningful today.

The *Department of Practical Theology's* . . . concern is to explore the work of the church in its various ministries and to relate those ministries to an understanding of the church, biblically, theologically, and sociologically.

The intellectual and theological interests of the Seminary were not limited to its degree programs. In the fall of 1962 the Center of Continuing Education was launched and held its first course in the recently acquired and later named Adams House. As churches adopted the policy of granting sabbatical and short leaves of absence to their clergy these courses grew in popularity to such an extent that within a short time over thirty conferences a year were held and within a decade there were as many as two thousand participants a year in the continuing education program that included both clergy and lay persons from various denominations. During these years the School of Christian Life and Leadership, sponsored by the Seminary, the Princeton Pastors Association, and the Churches of Greater Trenton, continued in the fall of each year its month-long Thursday evening training sessions on the campus for as many as three hundred from the surrounding churches.

In the sesquicentennial year of 1962–1963 a series of conferences on the campus were sponsored on the topics: Bible, Christian ethics, integrity of preaching, religion and psychiatry, religions of the world, and theology and philosophy. In that same year nine Soviet citizens were invited to participate in a conference that received some unexpected publicity because it was picketed by a group led by a graduate of the class of 1931.

In 1963–64, under the sponsorship of the World Student Christian Federation, a special program was conducted for twenty-six students from all continents who enrolled in courses at both the Seminary and the University. In the summer of 1964 selected students were given the opportunity of participating in a biblical archaeology project in the Near East. In May 1966 a conference financed by Edward F. Gallahue was held in Princeton at which Buddhists, Christians, Hindus, Jews and Muslims discussed "Religious Pluralism and World Community." On this occasion there were no pickets.

As the end of the 1960s approached, attention was given to the need for some students to have clinical experience in hospitals and health centers. In 1967 the Seminary joined in the creation of an association with New Jersey and Pennsylvania hospitals to operate a cooperative program in which a few students received clinical training and participated in quarterly seminars. Concurrent with this development the trustees appointed a committee to explore the possibility of merger with the New Brunswick Seminary, the result of which exploration was the approval of a plan for cross-registration by students of each seminary to enroll in selected courses in the other institution. At the same time a self-study report prepared for a re-accreditation review stated that to accommodate a growing number of non-Presbyterians the Seminary "has expanded its academic offerings so that the doctrinal and ecclesiastical education of these persons may be adequate for ordination in their own communions." It was further noted that their presence had also enriched the intellectual and social atmosphere of Princeton Seminary.

With the advent of the 1970s there was no diminution in academic initiatives. After abortive endeavors sixty years earlier a two-months long summer session was reinstated in 1971 in which one hundred students were registered that first year. With this second attempt the efforts proved to be successful since the summer school program has since been continuously operated on an annual basis. Concurrently with the Summer School a shorter summer language program was conducted for students wishing to become proficient in Greek and Hebrew. These two subjects had initially been offered in the summer for students who had in earlier years been required to attain proficiency to meet graduation requirements. In 1968 the language requirements for graduation had been revised and students were no longer required to include them in their regular undergraduate program. The stated rationale for this decision was that these courses demanded too much time which could be better employed for some students in pursuing other subjects in view of the explosion of knowledge.

INTER-INSTITUTIONAL COOPERATION

At the same time in 1971 cooperative arrangements were made with other institutions. One agreement was made with Beaver College in Jenkintown, Pennsylvania, in connection with the course in religious education which had in 1968 been reduced from three to two years. Enrollment in the program had been adversely affected by the eligibility of women to be ordained following their completion of the bachelor of divinity program. A second inter-institutional agreement provided the means by which a student in four years could obtain an undergraduate theology degree and the degree of Master of Social Work from Rutgers University.

Whereas neither of these two endeavors in inter-institutional cooperation involved many students, a third agreement was more significant. It reinforced the mutual benefits of cooperation with Princeton University and it renewed an earlier practice by which there was cross-registration in specific courses, as well as identification of one or more individuals from each institution as visiting professors in the other. This agreement coincided with the creation by the Seminary, the University and and four other local institutions of a procedure for cooperative purchasing.

In many respects the fourth inter-institutional agreement developed at this time represented more than a symbolic revision in theological attitudes. As a sequel to Vatican Council II the Roman Catholic Diocese of Trenton agreed to provide two visiting lecturers and to enroll at least twenty students at the Seminary each year in addition to employing the summer school for further study by its personnel engaged in religious education. The cordial relationship developed to such extent that in 1975 the Seminary and the Diocese celebrated the tenth anniversary of the Decree of Ecumenism when a mass was held in Miller Chapel with Johannes Cardinal Willebrands serving as the celebrant. But in time changes occur. With a new pope in Rome and a new bishop in Trenton the same spirit of ecumenical cooperation was pursued with less endorsement although Catholic students continued to enroll at the Seminary and Roman Catholics continued to be members of the faculty.

A fifth institution with which from its inception the Seminary has cooperated was the Center of Theological Inquiry. Commencing in the early 1980s the Center, long a dream of McCord, provided financial support and research facilities at first for two and then for a dozen or so scholars each year to pursue their advanced research on contemporary philosophical, theological and scientific issues. A building for the Center was constructed in 1984 on land contiguous to and purchased from the Seminary with the help of a major grant from the Henry Luce Foundation. As its second director, Daniel W. Hardy, successor to McCord, has stated—"the Center exists to promote the intelligent understanding of faith (theology) and to enhance its importance in academic, church and public life." With its separate endowment and its own board of trustees the Center has enjoyed many advantages, such as use of the Speer Library, by its physical proximity to the Seminary which in turn has gained from the intellectual and theological stimulation provided by the scholars in residence at the Center.

DEGREE NOMENCLATURE

The dynamics of theological education were further demonstrated by revisions in the names of degrees and in additional degree programs. In 1971 the American Association of Theological Schools had recommended to its member institutions that the first professional degree be the Master of Divinity. Accordingly, Princeton Seminary ceased to award the Bachelor of Divinity degree after 1971 (between 1921 and 1944 it had been Bachelor of Theology), and awarded the Master of Divinity for the same program. Graduates with the former bachelor's degree who wished to obtain the new master's degree could do so on payment of $25. Within a short time over one thousand alumnae and alumni availed themselves of this opportunity.

In 1972 the Master of Religious Education, first awarded in 1947, was supplanted by the Master of Arts degree that was initiated in 1973. At the same time the Doctor of Theology degree, which had been awarded since 1944, was replaced by the degree of Doctor of Philosophy with a reduction in the number of students admitted to the program whose areas of specialization were also reduced from thirteen to six. In addition to these changes a new degree program was added in 1972 leading to the degree of Doctor of Ministry in which a candidate could study four aspects of ministry: caring and restorative, communicative and educative, organizational and administrative, and theological and ethical. Each of these degree programs was subsequently continued as was the program leading to the Master of Theology degree, the only degree that has been offered continuously by the Seminary since its inception in 1921.

Aware of the social issues of the era and sensitive to the need to address them, the faculty of the Seminary with trustee support had expanded its program in field services so that by 1960 students were participating on week-ends in suburban and rural churches and involved in out-reach programs in Camden, Elizabeth, Newark, Philadelphia, Trenton and New York City. They did not overlook opportunities to exert a religious influence on the nearby campuses of Princeton and Rutgers universities, and Rider and Westminster Choir colleges. In the summer of that year twenty-one students served as interns in psychiatric hospitals in various sections of the United States. By 1965 the field education activities, which in 1988 became a mandatory part of the undergraduate curriculum, had become sufficiently well established to warrant a financial grant from the James Foundation. In 1973 a variation in the program was introduced when ten students, including one woman, resided, studied, and pursued their field work with the local churches and ethnic groups in Newark. Two members of the faculty commuted to provide instruction and supervision.

In this period the Seminary was also developing other special programs that included a program in black studies better to prepare students for service with black congregations, a program in women's studies, a program for military chaplains, and with the assistance of Princeton University a program to prepare students for teacher certification.

While the rate of academic innovation subsided in the 1980s there continued to be changes that became an integral part of the curricular offerings. In 1983 an agreement was established by which the adjacent Trinity Counseling Service provided instruction in the clinical pastoral education courses as well as clinical counseling services for individual students. With the growth in number of students from Asia, especially Korea, and with the growth of Korean-Presbyterian churches in the United States the Program for Asian-American Theology and Ministry was established that same year with generous financial assistance from churches and foundations. At the end of the decade two additional academic options were established. In one, a reciprocal arrangement was made with Westminster Choir College for inter-institutional course registration. In the other, a few students were provided the option of spending a semester in Washington in a program entitled the National Capital Semester for Seminarians.

EDUCATIONAL RESOURCES

With foresight, beginning with Archibald Alexander as the first librarian, Princeton Seminary has recognized the importance of a good library for sound theological learning. One of the major objectives has continued to be an up-to-date comprehensive collection of "the basic works of western and, in translation, eastern religious traditions." With its many special collections and its annual acquisitions the library continually expanded so that by 1990 it had over four hundred thousand volumes in addition to innumerable pamphlets and other documents. To handle the volume of work entailed in ordering, cataloguing, issuing, and receiving all these items the entire collection was recorded on computers commencing in 1985, the year before L. Charles Willard resigned from his eighteen year assignment as librarian to accept a position at Harvard University. He was succeeded by the respected former director of professional studies and registrar, James F. Armstrong '54, Helena Professor of Old Testament Language and Exegesis who, among his other responsibilities, coordinated plans for the construction, which was begun in 1992, of the Henry Luce III Library adjacent and connected to Speer Library.

Religious teaching and the transmission of religious ideas and thought has traditionally been through preaching to congregations and groups and through individual discussions. First cinema, then radio and television extended in an expansive way the opportunities for religion to extend its influence on a wider basis in society. Although in comparison to the newer charismatic denominations the Reformed churches have not been as enterprising in employing these newer media to serve their memberships, audio-visual services became an important adjunct to the education of students at Princeton Seminary. Stimulated largely by W. J. Beeners '48, first as an instructor in speech, the subsequent Media Resource Center under the supervision of Wayne R. Whitelock, director of Educational Communications and Technology, provided support to both the educational and administrative activities of the Seminary. Relocated in Templeton Hall when that building was completed in 1989 the center expanded its services to provide support for faculty in their classroom instruction, including homiletics, for students in their video endeavors, and for the administration with respect to conferences, special events, and public relations. This center, which is unsurpassed in its ability to serve its clientele, has maintained a library of some 6,500 recordings that have been loaned for use both on the campus and to alumni and others engaged in extending a religious influence to a wider audience.

Physically adjacent to the media center was located the computer center where students have had access to instruction in and the use of the equipment that has become a necessary tool in the educational process of research, learning, and writing.

CONTINUING EDUCATION

Completing its thirtieth year in 1992 the Center of Continuing Education continued throughout this period to offer "ministers and lay persons opportunities to participate further in ongoing theological inquiry to increase their effectiveness for the ministry." Supplementing the usual three-day sessions on the campus, the Center had in 1985 expanded its activities by sponsoring several travel seminars to such places as Africa and Central America.

In planning the programs its directors, who have included Jack Cooper '43 and Geddes W. Hanson '72, have been conscious of the fact that women and clergy from smaller parishes have participated less frequently, that other institutions have inaugurated competing programs similar to the program initiated at Princeton, and that in the midst of the affluence of the 1980s clergy had less available funds to engage in formal continuing education courses. Despite these facts continuing education at Princeton remained a significant program of intellectual renewal each year for thousands of men and women who had committed their lives to religious pursuits.

With a longer heritage than the Center of Continuing Education the Princeton Institute of Theology completed its fiftieth year in 1992. Enjoying wide appeal it had been forced by limitations of administrative and physical facilities to restrict enrollment in any one year to no more than three hundred.

Enrollment

As this historical account has already attested, trustees and faculty, administrative officers and staff, physical facilities and equipment, finances and loyal supporters have all been indispensable in the creation and the continued successful operation of Princeton Theological Seminary. But none of these essential components, singly or collectively, constitutes the reason for its existence. In 1808 Archibald Alexander, as Moderator of the General Assembly, urged the establishment of a seminary "for the single purpose of educating youth for the ministry." From its inception that was and has remained the primary purpose for Princeton Seminary. It is therefore fitting that its students and alumni should be the focus of attention in the final sections of this narrative history of the Seminary.

Whereas Princeton Theological Seminary has in recent years been one of the four largest seminaries in the United States, it has undergone fluctuations in the size of its enrollment and the number of candidates for admission. For a time in the early 1960s the enrollment seemed to have reached a plateau around five hundred, partially as a consequence of withdrawals of students whose vocational commitments changed. This situation stimulated a concerted effort at recruitment of candidates for

Edler Garnet Hawkins
Professor of Practical Theology from 1971 to 1977
and former Moderator of the General Assembly
conversing informally with students

the professional degree programs. Three-day vocational conferences, as they were called, were held each year to which prospective theological students were invited. By 1963, the third
year of these sessions, some three hundred and fifty were in
attendance. These efforts and general social factors resulted in
a steady increase in the enrollment at the Seminary.

By 1986 an appreciable decline in the number of applicants
for the Master of Divinity program was experienced in common
with most other seminaries. At Princeton the number of candidates in 1990, in comparison with ten years earlier, was forty-
six percent less, although the percentage of admitted students
of the total applications remained nearly the same, while there
was a sixteen percent reduction in the number of matriculants.
Despite fluctuations in enrollment Princeton Seminary in 1990
was educating twenty-seven percent of the students enrolled in
Master of Divinity programs in all Presbyterian related semi-

naries, two and one-half times more than the next largest Presbyterian seminary.

During these three decades certain features of the student body remained the same while other factors underwent gradual changes. Two dozen foreign countries continued to be represented each year by sixty to eighty students, the largest single number of which in the latter years were from Korea. The geographic distribution of domestic students continued to be very widespread with most states being represented each year while New Jersey, New York and Pennsylvania collectively provided the largest number. On the other hand, the number of different colleges and seminaries previously attended by the students doubled between 1960 and 1990. In the latter year the lists included 449 colleges and universities and 108 seminaries.

Of equal note was the fluctuation in the denominational affiliations of the students. Although from its early years the Seminary included students who were non-Presbyterians, in recent years these students have increased in both number and proportion. By 1972 there were more non-Presbyterians than members of the denomination by which the Seminary was founded, a situation that was reversed only temporarily as the last decade of the century began. Nevertheless, the denominations represented in the student body have numbered as many as seventy-four in 1987 when there were also forty-nine American blacks, ten Hispanics, and forty Asian-Americans.

Concurrent with these changes has been the rise in the average age of the student body. An analysis of the junior class in 1982 revealed that although sixty-two percent were under twenty-five years of age, twenty-one percent were between twenty-six and thirty, and seventeen percent were over thirty, some as old as fifty-one. The older men and women were students who were undertaking a second, or even a third career. Of more significance, forty percent were women. Four years later an analysis of the entire student body reported that forty-two percent were married of whom over one-half had children. These factors helped to intensify the financial pressure on the students who required both financial aid and work opportunities in order to meet their educational and family expenses.

Campus Life

In contrast to many other seminaries Princeton did not rely on the enrollment of students who selected the seminary because they could commute from home and thus benefit from reduced expenses. Princeton maintained a resident campus that provided a life of some excitement starting in the 1960s when so many campuses were in turmoil.

This was the era of frustrations, of protests, of deteriorating confidence in authority, when the student generation was convinced it was better able to rectify the ills of society. Caught between respect for the theological teachings of one's elders and religious idealism for a more perfect society, seminary students at Princeton, as well as at other institutions, relied on their own interpretations and in many cases acted on their own authority. Some withdrew from the Seminary, others fulfilled their required educational duties despite the distractions, and a few led protests both on and off the campus.

The forerunner of a later more dramatic protest occurred in 1968 when a dozen or more students instituted a sit-in at Speer Library over the issue of the hours of its closing. This act was terminated in a somewhat ludicrous manner. The activists, a few of whom were married, were advised that they would be locked in for the night when the building was closed at ten that evening. This possibility did not appeal to the wives who urged their husbands to desist. This early evening confrontation was easily resolved at an amicable conference the next morning. A temporary policy for later hours of closing for the library was adopted, and the new schedule permanently instituted the following fall.

Two years later a confrontation with the trustees produced a greater impact and provided ample evidence that students had opinions which they believed should be addressed by the governing body of the institution. When the board adjourned its meeting in Speer Library at 4:30 p.m. on May 5, 1970 the members were blockaded by students from leaving the building. Although a few trustees were able to escape through windows to fulfill other commitments the majority were incarcerated until 6:30 during which period negotiations were conducted by several trustees with three representatives of the student protestors. Their expressed concerns included the need for greater recognition of the interests of minorities, the war in Vietnam that had been extended into Cambodia, and a regular means of communication between students and trustees. In contrast to 1909 when the faculty protested vehemently over a written petition presented by the students to the trustees, in 1970 the students enjoyed the support of many professors, as well as an understanding on the part of the administration and many trustees.

The result of this incident was the creation of an official body, called the Princeton Seminary Conference, to include representatives of the trustees, faculty, administration, alumni, and students from each of the degree programs—a total of twenty-five individuals. Initially it met monthly and provided a regular means by which issues could be discussed in an open manner, issues that affected and were of concern to the major constituencies of the Seminary. The process also made it easier to resolve misunderstandings at a time when tensions were rife throughout society. As the years passed the need for this formal structure evaporated; it became difficult to obtain a quorum for meetings, and by 1985 the student governing body, the faculty, and the administration each voted that the Conference be discontinued. By this time student representatives were regularly serving on a number of faculty and academic departmental committees.

The demise of the Princeton Seminary Conference did not mean that there no longer were topics of concern to students. One may infer that later issues, such as those relating to the employment of inclusive language, association of black seminarians, the location of the women's center, campus security, and the lack of faculty attendance at the weekly chapel services, were not of such wide import that they distracted the entire student body from its usual campus life.

Whereas academic pursuits commanded most of the time of students, chapel services continued to be held each week-day morning, supplemented by small group prayer sessions and Bible discussions. Student deacons in married student apartments and each dormitory served under the supervision of the campus pastor who on occasion would sponsor student retreats.

Health services continued to be provided by the staff of Princeton University's infirmary, supplemented by a major medical insurance plan which was inaugurated in 1972 and in which each student was required to participate. Students were not required but encouraged to participate for both recreation and the benefit of their health in the informal intramural athletic program. And they could, if they individually chose, share with others in dramatic, literary, musical, and social activities.

Despite these many opportunities for mutual participation in cooperative activities it became increasingly difficult to maintain a feeling of campus solidarity beyond a generalized common religious commitment. The diversity of cultural, denominational, economic, national and racial backgrounds created in many ways a stimulating social environment. At the same time, as Michael E. Livingston '74, campus pastor and director of the chapel, observed, this diversity also encouraged the campus to be more combative over issues related to pluralism.

Fortunately, from time to time what dramatists call comic relief appeared on the campus to provide diversity of a different kind. J. Randall Nichols '67, director of the Doctor of Ministry program, reported that in the year of his graduation the drawing of a rat suddenly appeared one morning on the floor of the basement directly under the central stair-well of Hodge Hall. It had to do with strange gnawing sounds that developed each night and awakened one of the residents. "He was and is not known to be an immediately cheerful waker-upper. All efforts of the administration to exterminate action having failed, the matter was, so to speak, moved to the realm of the symbolic." Thus, "this low level protest (a pun) became a tradition and succeeding rats have appeared in various colors and hues" to the enjoyment of returning alumni and succeeding generations of students. (*PTS Alumni News*, 1984)

In another historical event a select group of alumnae and alumni, select because of their place of abode while students, were reminded of their campus life when in 1980 Hodge Hall was renovated. In the closet of room four hundred was revealed the list of residents in that room commencing in 1893 when the dormitory was constructed. The first name to be inscribed by the resident was that of James M. Farr, Jr. '94. The names of the first married couple were Ruth M. Thomas Sevier '49 and Fred M. Sevier '49 and the first single woman was Linda L. McCardle (Jaberg) '71. Before these and all the other names were painted over as part of the renovation process, they were photographed for a permanent record of this unusual list. Then, when the room was reoccupied later in the year the tradition was resumed on the same wall of the same closet.

Alumnae—Alumni

From analyses that were made of the graduates during the decade from 1980 to 1990 it was evident that the Seminary was continuing to fulfill its stated purpose of educating students to enter the ministry. Of the eighty percent of alumnae and alumni who responded seventy percent were engaged in pastorate pursuits or special ministries during their first year after graduation while another twenty percent were continuing graduate work. During that decade the yearly average of graduates from Princeton Seminary were 152 in the Master of Divinity program of which thirty-two percent were women, fifteen in the Master of Arts program of which sixty-one percent were women, fifty-four in the Master of Theology program of which twelve percent were women, and twelve in the Doctor of Philosophy program of which three percent were women. Most of those obtaining the doctoral degree became professors, educational administrators, or chaplains.

An earlier study made in 1977 in preparation for an accreditation visit reported that at that time the alumnae and alumni of Princeton comprised twenty-four percent of the active ministers of the United Presbyterian Church and that they were pastors of fifty-nine percent of the churches with congregations over two thousand. A similar study made ten years later indicated that at least eighty percent of the graduates remained in ministerial positions throughout their working lives. Of the

Graduation in 1966
Elinor Kirkland Hite being congratulated by her father, Bryant M.
Kirkland, with approval of Dean Athur M. Adams

then 9,370 living alumnae and alumni 814 were spread throughout the world, many having returned after their Princeton education to their native lands that included some seventy countries in Africa, Asia, Europe, and Latin America.

The earlier missionary influence that emanated from Princeton Theological Seminary extended the institution's reputation far and wide. This influence was enhanced in the middle of the twentieth century by such men as Samuel Hugh Moffett '42, who was born in Korea, the son of Samuel Austin Moffett, an early effective and influential missionary. After completing his education in the United States the younger Moffett returned to spend much of his life first in China and then in Korea as a professor and university administrator before becoming Professor of Ecumenics and Mission at Princeton. One of the impressive examples of this influence is Korea where in the early

1990s there were more Presbyterians than in all of the United States.

As a result of this missionary influence a succession of Koreans enrolled in Princeton Seminary and then returned to assume positions of influence as educators, pastors and leaders of their country. Among these men were Lak-Groon (Lark-June) George Paik '25, a university president; Kyung Chik Han '29, also a university president and founder of the Young Nak Church in Seoul with a stated membership of over sixty thousand; and Tien-Hsi Kao '55, a newspaper reporter, teacher and pastor who was at one time a political prisoner. Among the many others were three Moons, each of whom became a teacher: Peter Chan Kyu Moon '33, Stephen Tongwhan Moon '55, at one time also a political prisoner, and Timothy Ikwhan Moon '56.

Social protest by Princeton alumni was not limited to Korea. Samuel Sourinay Makary '55, an Egyptian Coptic bishop, suffered imprisonment in Ethiopa. In the United States Eugene Carson Blake '33 led protest marches against racism and McCarthyism for which he underwent arrest on several occasions. In the 1960s students with members of the faculty and administration participated in the march in Alabama to protest discrimination. James J. Reeb '53 was killed in the protest march against racial discrimination in Selma, Alabama, on March 11, 1965 . This event was reminiscent of the murder in 1837 of Elijah P. Lovejoy, class of 1834, in Alton, Illinois, following his newspaper articles opposing slavery.

Whereas these actions were intended to improve public attitudes and accordingly received much publicity, most alumni were performing their responsibilities of religious education and leadership in a manner befitting the traditional concepts of a pastor. Similarly alumnae in growing numbers were quietly assuming positions of responsibility in various capacities.

In its first one hundred and sixty years, that is through 1972, the Seminary awarded degrees to sixty-two women, many of whom had been enrolled in the Christian education program. By 1991 over 1,300 degrees had been granted to women in all programs with the largest number awarded in any one year being eighty in 1987. Among these alumnae were Sharon Elaine Rise '64, the first alumna to be elected an alumnae trustee, and Karen Turner McClellan '76, the first clergywoman trustee. F. Diana Pohlman Bell had the unusual distinction of being the first woman navy chaplain, serving in the naval reserve on her graduation from the Seminary in 1973. Although some denominations and other religions continue to prohibit women from serving in a ministerial capacity, Princeton Theological Seminary, as well as all Presbyterians in general, have gained immeasurably from the acceptance and recognition of women in positions of equality.

To coordinate and support the continued interest of the alumnae and alumni in the welfare of the Seminary, the Alumni-Alumnae Association was reorganized in the 1970s and again in the 1980s to provide for the establishment of regional chapters with their own officers and executive councils, similar in structure to the national council. In 1961 the *Alumni-Alumnae News* was established to supplement the *Princeton Seminary Bulletin* which was initiated in 1907. Copies of each of these publications have subsequently and regularly been mailed to all members of the Association, membership in which has been open to all alumnae and alumni for whom no dues have been assessed. At the time of writing this history Dean E. Foose '64 has been serving as Alumni-ae Secretary and Director of Placement in which latter position he has been providing invaluable assistance both to graduating students but also to alumni and alumnae who may for any number of reasons wish to be relocated. The Secretary also has had the responsibility of organizing the annual meetings of the Association which have been held prior to commencement and which have been attended by various members of the administration and the faculty.

Addressing an alumnae-alumni gathering in 1983 Hugh T. Kerr, Jr., then Benjamin B. Warfield Professor of Systematic Theology, spoke on the subject of "The Vision to Keep Moving Beyond." Kerr, an editor of *Theology Today* from its founding in 1944 until his death in 1992 , observed that "the Seminary encourages believers to be scholars, and scholars to be believers." Then addressing the issue of the future of Princeton Theological Seminary, he commented—

Blessed with many resources, including an honored heritage, and ecumenical faculty and student body, a world famous library, a beautiful campus in an academic community, and a significant endowment, this legacy becomes the basis for hope as the Seminary moves in confidence toward the future.

For Thomas W. Gillespie, president of the Seminary, its future is based on the unity that emanates from the Holy Spirit and "a theology which affirms the good news, clarifies our understanding of the good news, and makes it possible for people to embrace the good news with deep conviction."

Epilogue

Princeton Theological Seminary into
the Twenty-First Century

Among the many aphorisms uttered by John A. Mackay was the observation that "the road to tomorrow leads through yesterday." Most yesterdays are forgotten except by the historians and they inevitably tend to concentrate their attention on a segment of history unrelated to developments of other periods that may provide explanations of subsequent events. An example pertinent to this narrative history is the vivid description of the founders of the College of New Jersey provided by its historian, Thomas J. Wertenbaker.

To the little group who accomplished this great work—Dickinson, Burr, Edwards, the Tennents, Davies, Finley and others—latter-day Princetonians must accord gratitude and respect. It is not easy for the present age to understand the psychology of these men, to brush aside the changes of the two centuries and think with their minds, feel with their hearts, tremble with their fears. To many today the spectacle of a Gilbert Tennent in the pulpit, threatening his auditors with eternal damnation and driving scores to despair, is an unlovely one. But if we understand that Tennent had devoted his life to rescuing souls—that as the physician must warn his patient of the progress of disease so he considered it his duty to warn of the fatal progress of sin, that he would willingly have undergone privation, hardship, death itself to save the humblest from the burning—we glimpse the real man. (Wertenbaker, *Princeton*, p. 46)

The religious convictions of these men—the founders of the College of New Jersey—were shared by their theological descendants who were responsible only a few years later for the creation of the Seminary of the Presbyterian Church. It was they—Archibald Alexander, Ashbel Green and Samuel Miller—whose conception of an institution to educate the clergy with vital piety and sound educational learning was implemented in 1812 and then maintained with a conservative adherence and vigor that has affected in various degrees all subsequent students and faculty at the Seminary.

It is this tradition that motivated Robert Elliott Speer to declare when lecturing in Scotland in 1910:

But Christianity must continue, and all the more as this transformation advances, to seek to win individual men away from their religions to Christianity. If by proselytizing is meant winning men from all that is false and evil in the world's religions and relating them to the one universal religion, which is all truth and good, in other words, the effort to make Hindus and Mohammedans Christians, then that is just what we are trying to do. We are proselytizing. And we do not see what else in the world is worth doing. (Wood, p. 22)

Repeating this same theme soon after his arrival from Europe nearly thirty years later Otto A. Piper emphasized the supremacy of Christianity when he addressed a regional conference of the American Association of Theological Schools held on the Princeton Seminary campus in May 1939. In his speech on "Protestantism and World Cultures" he stated:

Christian religion would not be able to transform the structure of civilization and culture if it were one of those "natural" forms of religion that accompany the various types of civilization.

In our Christian belief we embrace a truth which is superior to all other views of the world and of human nature . . .

Thus evangelism is superior to all education and cultural, social, political, and economic activities.

These religious convictions and similar convictions in other faiths and denominations have been an undergirding force in society from the time humans first believed in and worshipped an Unseen Being. These convictions have stimulated a cohesive commitment and loyalty among people who have developed and have adhered to a common belief which they become convinced is superior to any other. At the same time, these convictions have also led to strife, schisms, and armed warfare, even on the part of a religion that teaches pacifism and peaceful resolution of disputes.

In its one hundred and eighty year history Princeton Seminary has been affected by and involved in the struggles with such divisive issues as enlightenment or pietism, reason or revelation, religion or science, and individual salvation or social welfare. Now the Seminary is again confronted with the issue of denominationalism or ecumenism, a word in itself which is subject to many interpretations and thus can be divisive.

In 1948 Joyce O. Hertzler, then a professor of sociology at the University of Nebraska, wrote—

Religion is one phase of man's cultural system—a body of attitudes, ideas, and techniques—whereby he explains and adjusts himself to the unknown, the mysterious, and the mighty. . . .

The most sinister fact, though, is that it is easier to administer the affairs of an organization than it is to keep creeds flexible, codes of conduct clear and uncompromised and the life of the spirit imminent. Historically this has meant either the eventual disappearance of the particular religious organization or, more commonly, reform or schism, especially in the form of new sects and cults. (Hertzler)

Near the end of the twentieth century when nationalism and tribalism are spreading throughout the world like a pandemic, and when peoples are seeking refuge in denominationalism and sectarianism, the pressures on theological educators at such institution as Princeton Theological Seminary are immense. The statement known as the Confession of 1967 developed by a committee, whose chairman was the Princeton Seminary professor, Edward A. Dowey, Jr., and which was adopted by the United Presbyterian Church, formally expanded the field of Presbyterian theology to include "the whole of man's life: social and cultural, economic and political, scientific and technological, individual and corporate." Within this broad mandate how will Princeton Seminary, as it approaches the twenty-first century, resolve the tensions that are inherent between denominationalism and ecumenism?

From a global point of view Benjamin R. Barber, professor of political science at Rutgers University, has uttered a word of caution.

Whatever forms of Enlightenment universalism might once have come to grace such historically related forms of monotheism as Judaism, Christianity, and Islam, in many of their modern incarnations they are parochial rather than cosmopolitan, angry rather than loving, proselytizing rather than ecumenical, zealous rather than rationalistic, sectarian rather than deistic, ethnocentric rather than universalizing.

As a result, the new forms of hypernationalism, the new expressions of religious fundamentalism are fractious and pulverizing, never integrating. (Barber)

With a faculty that includes men and women from different Christian denominations, with a student body comprised of married and unmarried men and women of different ages, different cultures, different nationalities, different races, and different religions, the Seminary enjoys both the grave responsibility and the immense opportunity of balancing the tensions that are inherent in this congregation of individuals who share a common commitment—a commitment to the salvation of the individual and to the betterment of life for all men and women wherever they may live.

Bibliography

Ahlstrom, Sydney E., *A Religious History of the American People*, New Haven: Yale University Press, 1972

Alexander, George, "The Glory of the Ministry," *Princeton Seminary Bulletin*, November 1927

Alexander, James W., *Forty Years' Familiar Letters*, New York: Charles Scribner's Sons, 1860

————, *The Life of Archibald Alexander, D.D.*, New York: Charles Scribners and Sons, 1854

Armstrong, Maurice W., Lefferts A. Loetscher, Charles A. Anderson, Editors, *The Presbyterian Enterprise*, Philadelphia: Westminster Press, 1956

Barber, Benjamin R., "Jihad vs. McWorld," *Atlantic*, March 1992

Barker, William S. "The Social Views of Charles Hodge (1797–1878): A Study in 19th Century Calvinism and Conservatism," *Covenant Seminary Review*, Spring 1975

The Benham Club—History, 1879–1895, Princeton Seminary, 1895

Billington, Ray A., *The Protestant Crusade, 1800–1860*, New York: Macmillan Company, 1938

Brief History of the Theological Seminary of the Presbyterian Church at Princeton, New Jersey, together with the Constitution, By-Laws, &c., Princeton: Printed by John Bogart, 1838

Brown, William A., "A Century of Theological Education and After," *Journal of Religion*, July 1926

————, *The Education of American Ministers—Volume I—Ministerial Education in America—Summary and Interpretation*, New York: Institute of Social and Religious Research, 1934

Calhoun, David B., *The Last Command—Princeton Theological Seminary and Missions, 1812–1862*, Doctoral dissertation, Princeton Theological Seminary, 1983

Chinard, Gilbert, "A Landmark in American Intellectual History, *Princeton University Library Chronicle*, Winter 1953

Clutter, Ronald T., *The Reorientation of Princeton Theological Seminary, 1900–1929*, Doctoral dissertation, Dallas Theological Seminary, 1982

Coalter, Milton J., Jr., *Gilbert Tennent, Son of Thunder—A Case Study of Continental Pietism's Impact on the First Great Awakening in the Middler Colonies*, Westport: Greenwood Press, 1987

Coalter, Milton J., John W. Mulder, and Louis B. Weeks, Editors, *The Presbyterian Predicament: Six Perspectives*, Louisville: Westminster-John Knox Press, 1990

Craighead, J. G., *Scotch and Irish Seeds in American Soil*, Philadelphia: Presbyterian Board of Publications, 1878

Drummond, Andrea L., *Story of American Protestantism*, Edinburgh: Oliver and Boyd, 1951

Dulles, J. H., "Princeton Theological Seminary," *The History of Education in New Jersey*, David Murray, Editor, 1903

Gapp, Kenneth S., "The Theological Seminary Library," *Princeton University Library Chronicle*, Winter 1954

Gaustad, Edwin S., *Dissent in American Religion*, University of Chicago Press, 1973

————, *A Religious History of America*, New York: Harper and Row, 1966

————, Editor, *Religious Issues in American History*, New York: Harper and Row, 1968

General Assembly of the Presbyterian Church in the U.S.A., *Plan of the Theological Seminary of the Presbyterian Church in the United States of America, Located at Princeton, New Jersey*, Adopted in 1811, and amended by subsequent Assemblies

————, *Reports Relation to Princeton Theological Seminary*, St. Paul, Minnesota, 1929

Gillespie, Thomas W., "The Three Faces of Evangelism," speech presented at the Moderators Conference on Evangelism, Princeton Theological Seminary, April 16, 1986

Gillett, E. H., *History of the Presbyterian Church*, Philadelphia: Presbyterian Publications Committee, 1864

Green, Ashbel, "Theological Seminary at Princeton, N.J.," *The Christian Advocate*, February 1825

Hageman, John F., *History of Princeton and Its Institutions, Two Volumes*, Philadelphia: J.B. Lippincott and Company, 1879

Handy, Robert T., *A History of Union Theological Seminary in New York*, New York: Columbia University Press, 1987

Harbison, Janet, "John Mackay of Princeton," *Presbyterian Life*, September 15, 1958 and October 1, 1958

Hardy, Daniel W., "Theological Inquiry Today," speech to the Old Guard of Princeton, January 9, 1991

Hart, John W., "Princeton Theological Seminary: The Reorganization of 1929," *Journal of Presbyterian History*, Summer 1980

Hertzler, Joyce O., "Religious Institutions," *The Annals of the American Academy of Political and Social Science*, March 1948

Hodge, Archibald A., *The Life of Charles Hodge*, New York: Charles Scribner's Sons, 1880

Hodge, Charles, *Proceedings of the Semi-Centennial Celebration of the Theological Seminary*, New York: Anson D.F. Randolph and Company, 1872

————, *Systematic Theology*, Grand Rapids, Michigan, Wm. B. Eerdmans Publishing Company, Reprinted 1977, 3 volumes

Hoeveler, R. David, *James McCosh and the Scottish Intellectual Tradition— From Glasgow to Princeton*, Princeton University Press, 1981

Hoffecker, W. Andrew, *Piety and the Princeton Theologians—Archibald Alexander, Charles Hodge, and Bejmanin Warfield*, Grand Rapids: Baker Book House, 1981

Jones, Charles A. III, *Charles Hodge—The Keeper of Orthodoxy: The Method, Purpose and Meaning of His Apologetic*, Doctoral dissertation, Drew University, 1989

Kelly, Robert L., *Theological Education in America—A Study of 161 Theological Schools in United States and Canada*, New York: George H. Doran Company, 1924

Kemeny, Paul C., "President Francis Landey Patton, Princeton University, and Faculty Ferment, *American Presbyterians*, Summer 1991

Kerr, Hugh T., "Over the Years—A Personal Perspective, May, 1991 (duplicated statement)

———, "The Seminary and the College: The First Twenty-Five Years," *Princeton Seminary Bulletin*, Vol. VI, No. 1

———, Editor, *Sons and Prophets—Leaders in Protestantism from Princeton Seminary*, Princeton University Press, 1963

Kuklick, Bruce, *Churchmen and Philosophers—From Jonathan Edwards to John Dewey*, New Haven: Yale University Press, 1958

Leitch, Alexander, *A Princeton Companion*, Princeton University Press, 1978

Lenox, James, "Extract from Deed of Property to Princeton Theological Seminary, May 5, 1843," Files of Seminary business records

Link, Arthur S., Editor, *The First Presbyterian Church of Princeton—Two Centuries of History*, Princeton University Press, 1967

Loetscher, Lefferts A., *A Brief History of the Presbyterians*, Philadelphia: Westminster Press, 1983 (4th edition)

———, *The Broadening Church—A Study of Theological Issues in the Presbyterian Church since 1869*, Philadelphia: University of Pennsylvania Press, 1954

———, *Facing the Enlightenment and Pietism—Archibald Alexander and the Founding of Princeton Theological Seminary*, Westport: Greenwood Press, 1983

Longfield, Bradley J., *The Presbyterian Controversy—Fundamentalists, Modernists, and Moderates*, New York: Oxford University Press, 1989

Macartney, Clarence E., *The Log College and the Beginning of Princeton*, Sermon preached at First Presbyterian Church, Pittsburgh, Pennsylvania, May 19, 1946

Mackay, John, "Letter to Presbyterians," October 21, 1953

Maclean, John, *History of the College of New Jersey*, Philadelphia: J. B. Lippincott and Company, 1877

Massa, Conrad H., "Confessional Churches and Their Theological Institutions," *The Princeton Seminary Bulletin*, Vol. XII, No. 3, 1991

Miller, Donald G., *The Scent of Eternity—A Life of Harris Elliott Kirk of Baltimore*, Macon: Mercer University Press, 1989

Miller, Glenn T., *Piety and Intellect—The Aims and Purposes of Ante-Bellum Theological Education*, Atlanta: Scholars Press, 1990

Miller, Howard, *The Revolutionary College—American Presbyterian Higher Education, 1707–1837*, New York University Press, 1976

Miller, Samuel, Jr., *The Life of Samuel Miller*, Philadelphia: Claxton, Remsen and Haffelfinger, 1869

Miller, Samuel H., "Church, Seminary and the World—An Uneasy Frontier," *Theological Education*, Summer 1966

Miller, William S. "Presbyterian Signers of the Declaration of Independence," *Journal of the Presbyterian Historical Society*, September 1958

Morrill, Guy L. *Your Presbyterian Church*, Auburn: Hubbard Press, 1926

Moseley, James G., *A Cultural History of Religion in America*, Westport: Greenwood Press, 1981

Mulder, John M. and John F. Wilson, editors, *Religion in American History—Interpretive Essays*, Englewood Cliffs: Prentice-Hall, 1978

Nichols, James H., *Romanticism in American Theology*, University of Chicago Press, 1961

Noll, Mark A., "Before the Storm—Life at Princeton College, 1806–1807," *Princeton University Library Chronicle*, No. 3, 1980–1981

———, "The Founding of Princeton Seminary," *The Westminster Theological Journal*, Vol. 42, 1979–1980

———, "Jacob Green's Proposal for Seminaries," *Journal of Presbyterian History*, Fall 1980

———, *Princeton and the Republic—The Search for a Christian Enlightenment in the Era of Samuel Stanhope Smith 1768–1822*, Princeton University Press, 1989

———, *The Princeton Theology, 1812–1921—Scripture, Science, and Theological Method from Archibald Alexander to Benjamin Breckenridge Warfield*, Grand Rapids: Baker Book House, 1983

———, "The Princeton Trustees of 1807: New Men and New Directions," *Princeton University Library Chronicle*, 1979–1980, No. 3

Osgood, Charles G., *Lights in Nassau Hall—Princeton 1746–1946*, Princeton University Press, 1951

Presbyterian Encyclopedia of the Presbyterian Church, 1884

Presbyterian Reunion: Memorial Volume—1837–1871, New York: DeWitt C. Lent and Company, 1870

Princeton Theological Seminary, *Biographical Catalogues*, 1818, 1909, 1932, 1954, 1977

———, *Catalogues of the Seminary*, 1821 and succeeding years

———, *General Catalogues of Alumni*, 1862 and 1872

———, *Institutional Self-Study Reports*, 1968, 1977, 1987

———, Minutes, Board of Directors, 1812–1929

————, Minutes, Board of Trustees, 1826–1991

————, *Necrology of Princeton Seminary, 1875–1932* (six volumes)

————, *Princeton Seminary Bulletins*, 1907 and succeeding years

————, *The Princeton Spire*, 1961 and succeeding years

————, *P. T. S. Alumni News*, 1959 and succeeding years

Princeton University, Minutes of the Board of Trustees, 1805–1815, and "Memorandum Relating to the Relations Between Princeton Theological Seminary and Princeton University," January 11, 1934

Purves, George T., "The Theological Seminary," *The Princeton Book*, Boston: Houghton, Osgood and Company, 1879

Rian, Edwin H., *The Presbyterian Conflict*, Grand Rapids: William B. Eerdmans Publishing Company, 1940

Roberts, William H., *The Ecclesiastical Status of the Theological Seminaries*, Cincinnati: Herald and Presbyter Print, 1892

————, "Library of the Theological Seminary," *The Princeton Book*, Boston: Houghton, Osgood and Company, 1879

Rogers, Robert W., "What Should Be the Ideals of the Theological Seminary for Usefulness in the Coming Half-Century?" *McCormick Theological Seminary—Historical Recognition of 80th Year in 1909*, Chicago: Lakeside Press

Ruether, Rosemary and Eleanor McLaughlin, Editors, *Women of Spirit—Female Leadership in the Jewish and Christian Traditions*, New York: Simon and Schuster, 1979

Ryan, Halford R., *Harry Emerson Fosdick—Persuasive Preacher*, Westport: Greenwood Press, 1989

Salmond, C. A., *Princetoniana: Charles and A. A. Hodge, with Class and Table Talk of Hodge the Younger*, New York: Charles Scribner's Sons, 1888

Sandeen, Ernest R., "The Princeton Theology—One Source of Biblical Liberalism in American Protestanism," *Church History*, September 1962

Schisler, Charles H., *A History of Westminster Choir College*, Doctoral dissertation, Indiana University, 1976

Scott, Donald M., *From Office to Profession, The New England Ministry—1750–1850*, Philadelphia: University of Pennsylvania Press, 1978

Scott, William B., *Some Memories of a Paleontologist*, Princeton University Press, 1939

Selden, William K., *The Legacy of John Cleve Green*, Princeton University: Office of Printing Services, 1988

————, *The Princeton Summer Camp—1908–1975*, Princeton Education Center at Blairstown, 1987

Smith, Elwyn A., "The Evolution of Purpose in American Theological Education," *Theological Education*, Winter 1966

Speer, Robert E., "Princeton In the Mission Field," *Princeton Seminary Bulletin*, June 1935

Stevenson, J. Ross, *The Historical Position of Princeton Seminary*, privately printed, 1928

Sweet, William W., *Religion in the Development of American Culture*, New York: Charles Scribner's Sons, 1952

——, "The Rise of Theological Schools in America," *Church History*, September 1937

Thorp, Willard, *The Lives of Eighteen from Princeton*, Princeton University Press. 1946

Trinterud, Leonard J., *The Forming of an American Tradition—A Re-examination of Colonial Presbyterianism*, Philadelphia: Westminster Press, 1949

Warfield, Benjamin B., *The Expansion of the Seminary—A Historical Sketch*, Princeton: Published Privately by Order of the Board of Directors, 1914

——, "How Princeton Seminary Got to Work," *Journal of the Presbyterian Historical Society*, June 1918

——, "Notes on Certain Proposed Readjustments of the Curriculum," 1914 (Independently printed)

——, *The Westminster Assembly and Its Work*, New York: Oxford University Press, 1931

Wells, David F., editor, *Reformed Theology in America—A History of Modern Development*, Grand Rapids: William B. Eerdmans Publishing Company. 1986

Wertenbaker, Thomas J., "The College of New Jersey and the Presbyterians," *Journal of the Presbyterian Historical Society*, December 1958

——, *The Founding of American Civilization—The Middle Colonies*, New York: Charles Scribner's Sons, 1938

——, *Princeton, 1746–1896*, Princeton University Press, 1946

Willis-Watkins, E. David, "Systematic Theology by Charles Hodge," *Journal of Presbyterian History*, Winter 1988

Wilson, Stanton R., *Studies in the Life and Work of an Ecumenical Churchman—Studies of John Mackay*, Master of Theology dissertation, Princeton Theological Seminary, 1958

Wood, Forrest G., *The Arrogance of Faith*, New York: Alfred A. Knopf, 1990

Index

The Author

Ever since his graduation from Princeton University in 1934 William K. Selden, a native of Oil City, Pennsylvania, pursued his interest in higher education at a succession of institutions. Following administrative positions at Princeton, Brown and Northwestern universities, he was president of Illinois College, a Congregational and Presbyterian affiliated institution. He then moved to Washington, D.C. as executive director of the National Commission on Accrediting in which position he assisted in the merger of the American Association of Schools of Religious Education and the American Association of Theological Schools. Subsequently he was vice president of The American Assembly at Columbia University before undertaking a number of consulting assignments in higher education at the national, regional and state levels. More recently he has pursued a second career as an historian of institutions in the Princeton community. Although raised as an Episcopalian, when a resident of Illinois he served as a deacon in the First Presbyterian Church of Evanston, and as an elder in the First Presbyterian Church of Jacksonville. Subsequently he served as a member of the Advisory Committee on Colleges and the Advisory Panel on College Appropriations of the Board of Christian Education of the United Presbyterian Church. Among his earlier writings was *The Legacy of John Cleve Green*, a trustee and one of the largest donors to Princeton Theological Seminary in the 19th century.